Another Look AT Life FROM A Deer Stand

Going Deeper into the Woods

Steve Chapman

HARVEST HOUSE PUBLISHERS

EUGENE, OREGON

Except where otherwise indicated, Scripture quotations in this book are taken from the New American Standard Bible®, © 1960, 1962, 1963, 1968, 1971, 1972, 1973, 1975, 1977 by The Lockman Foundation. Used by permission. (www.Lockman.org)

Verses marked NKJV are taken from the New King James Version. Copyright ©1982 by Thomas Nelson, Inc. Used by permission. All rights reserved.

Verses marked KJV are taken from the King James Version of the Bible.

Italics in Scripture quotations indicate author's emphasis.

Illustrations by Steve Chapman

Cover Photo © Charles Alsheimer

Cover by Koechel Peterson & Associates, Inc., Minneapolis, Minnesota

ANOTHER LOOK AT LIFE FROM A DEER STAND

Text and illustrations copyright © 2007 by Steve Chapman
Published by Harvest House Publishers
Eugene, Oregon 97402
www.harvesthousepublishers.com

Library of Congress Cataloging-in-Publication Data
Chapman, Steve.
    Another look at life from a deer stand / Steve Chapman.
       p. cm.
    Originally published: Madison, TN: S&A Family, Inc.; 1996.
    ISBN-13: 978-0-7369-1891-6
    ISBN-10: 0-7369-1891-4
      1. White-tailed deer hunting—Anecdotes—Tennessee.   2. Conduct of life—Anecdotes.
    3. Chapman, Steve.   I. Title.
    SK301.C514   1998
    799.2'7652'092—DC21   97-42832

Printed in the United States of America

07 08 09 10 11 12 13 14 15 / BP-SK / 10 9 8 7 6 5 4 3 2

Contents

On the Trail of Truth

As the late evening sun slowly fell behind the western horizon, I reluctantly prepared to climb down from my tree stand. While I unbuckled the wrist strap that held the mechanical bowstring release to my hand, I continued to check the area for incoming deer. I knew it was too dark to take a shot, but I never like to get caught exiting a stand by the local whitetails. Anything I can do to avoid educating a deer about the hiding places I have picked out is a good thing. Feeling sure that I was alone, I headed to the ground. But I wasn't alone.

When I detached the bow from the hoisting string and turned to walk to my truck, I had not taken but five steps when I heard the troubling sound of escaping deer crashing through the crisp, dry leaves. I knew that once more the sun had set 15 minutes too soon.

Because my timing was off…again…it was another disappointing evening of deer hunting. It wasn't a super let down though because I had a great time trying. I'm never, ever saddened by the attempt. Instead, I felt somewhat downhearted because so many days of the season had passed, and my tag was yet to be punched. There were deer in the area, but over and over they weren't showing up while I still had shooting light.

The problem was that I was young at hunting with a bow, and there was a bit of archery hunting wisdom I hadn't discovered. What I didn't know was hurting me. However, that would soon change when I shared my recurring dilemma with a more experienced bow hunter. I mentioned him in my first book, *A Look at Life from a Deer Stand*. His name is Mark Smith. His advice was short on words but really long on profound insight.

"You're not going deep enough in the woods, good buddy," Mark said with his Louisiana drawl.

"I'm not what?" I asked.

"You probably like the edge of the field 'cause it's easier, plus you probably like it 'cause the light hangs on a little longer."

"Well, you're right about the light thing," I said and then countered with, "but I can't say that I set up near the field edges 'cause it's easy. I do it 'cause the deer like to come to the fields in the evening to browse. They're always arriving late though."

Mark smiled as I spoke, as if he already knew what to say. When I finished my whining he said, "That's just my point. The deer you're hunting are smart critters. They'll hang back in the woods until it's dark enough for them to feel safe to go out into the open. This is especially true for the bigger, more mature bucks. If you want to get an arrow into one of the whitetails on that farm, you're gonna have to take your climber farther back into the woods and catch them earlier in their trip to the soybeans."

What Mark said made so much sense that I nearly hugged him. But because I don't like getting beat up, I kept my arms to myself. I just thanked him profusely. Seriously, when another hunter shares the kind of revelation Mark provided for me that day, I get all razzed up...and I actually will struggle to sleep until I can give it a try.

Sure enough, Mark was right. An evening or two later I was able to head back to the farm. I relocated my portable climber about 75 yards farther back into the timber. About 15 minutes before the woods turned too dark to legally shoot, which is always much sooner than at the field edge in the early part of the season, a trio of sizable deer came casually strolling under my stand. They had exited their bedding area among the clutter of cut, fallen treetops and were slowly heading toward the soybeans. Just as the light finally went out inside the woods I found the doe I arrowed lying a mere 40 yards from the tree where I had placed my climber.

I can't say that a season has gone by since then that I don't remember Mark's suggestion. It revolutionized my approach to deer hunting. While I still like the field edges for its relative ease and the extra shooting light that it yields as the sun sets, I know that if several days go by without sightings or success, it's time to change my tactics by going deeper. This is especially true when it comes to pursuing the really mature whitetail bucks.

When Mark shared the fruit of his hunting experience with me in the early 1980s, he didn't know that his wisdom would also contribute to my spiritual life. I have thought of his words from time to time when I sense a need to pursue the heavier trophies of truth in God's written Word. There are times when I am aware that a few morning minutes in a brief, glancing study of a passage will not be enough. I know I might need to spend an hour, even hours in study and meditation in order to gain in-depth insights.

Please don't misunderstand me about engaging in short devotionals. In no way do I discount the importance of a quick daily read. In fact, I believe so strongly they can be a very important part of a complete breakfast for spiritual champions that I have written several hunting and fishing devotionals to meet the need. However, when there is a sense of emptiness in the spirit and an intense hunger for the meatier truths of the Scriptures, it is time to go deeper into the woods of the Word.

Through the years there have been many insights I've harvested by going further inside the Word. How thankful I am that a good number of them have been found while in the deer stand. The book you hold in your hands contains some trophies of truth, and I sincerely hope you not only enjoy reading about them but that you'll be inspired by them. And more important, if you sense a hunger to find the heavier truths available in God's Word, I hope this book will motivate you to not just hunt the edges of the field but to intentionally go deeper into the timber of the Scriptures.

Blessings on all your seasons. Happy hunting!

Steve Chapman

1

Good Waiting

After a season closes, deer hunters wait on average eight long months for the opening day of the next season. With so many days on the calendar to put our x's through, it's no wonder that those of us who cherish the hunt have a lot of trouble leaving the woods at the end of that first day. But the reluctance to exit a stand doesn't stop on opening day for me. Throughout the season leaving the woods is rarely something I want to do. A meeting that can't be postponed, a flight to catch, looming darkness, lightning bolts, loggers taking the tree I'm sitting in, a son or daughter getting married, and another season closing are just a few reasons to have to wrap up the day and head to the house. Though I am very much aware that I can easily make trouble for myself if I don't go home when I need to, I am very often guilty of trying to squeeze as many minutes in the deer stand as I possibly can.

This "short" in my wiring has been sparking for a long time. I recall when I was 16 years old and deer hunting in the McClintic Wildlife Station north of Point Pleasant, West Virginia. I stayed on a ground stand until I couldn't see the sights at the end of my .30-30 barrel, which was a short carbine, hardly 20 inches long. I unwillingly stood up and, because I didn't have a light, I began the stumble back to the gravel road where my folks' car was parked.

As I neared the Chevy that was light green in color and sort of softly glowed in the evening blackness, I thought I saw the dark form of a human standing next to it. I halted. The form didn't move...I didn't move. The silhouette and I were in a standoff. I gripped my rifle tightly and very slowly began to raise it to my hip. My heart rate shot up, and I gasped for breath as I searched for the hammer with my thumb. I pressed on it gently and waited in full alert.

Suddenly the silhouette spoke.

"Gettin' back to your vehicle a little late, aren't you, Mister?"

Obviously the title "mister" that I was given revealed the stranger didn't know he was facing down a kid who was trembling from head to toe like a nervous Barney Fife. I swallowed hard and offered as confident a reply as I could muster.

"Yep."

Any more words than one and the tremble in my voice would have been easily detected.

"Is there a reason you're so late?"

"Is there a reason you're asking?" I shot back.

That's when the flashlight abruptly came on. Little did I know, as I stood there totally blinded by the light he must have taken from the front end of a locomotive, I had just challenged the integrity and authority of a game warden.

When he got a good look at me and my stance with the rifle he must have seen that I was tense and needed a bit of calming.

"Young man, I'm an officer with the West Virginia

Department of Natural Resources, and I must ask you, Is that rifle still loaded?"

"Yes, Sir." (Somehow my manners returned!)

"Then please unload it right there where you're standing."

"Yes, Sir."

As I put the four cartridges in my jacket and dug through my pants pockets for my license, I explained to the officer that the reason I was so late getting to the car was that I really liked to wait as long as I could before leaving the stand. He was very kind to listen to my excuse, but he showed no sympathy as he offered a brief but stern lecture about the dangers of being alone in the woods after dark. Thankfully he sent me on my way without further consequences.

I'd like to report that his warning did some good, but quite honestly it didn't connect. To this day I'm still likely to wait until the last possible millisecond before leaving a deer stand. But the good news is I think I finally figured out the main reason I'm wired in such a weird way. It's because I enjoy "good" *waiting*.

Like most Americans these days, I do enough waiting that is tedious. You know, the kind that yields little in the way of delight. For example, I frequently get in airport security checkpoint lines where the only happy people present are those who have never flown or haven't flown since September 11, 2001 (rare birds they are!). They seem to be totally oblivious to the fact that their waiting might result in being randomly chosen for a complete body cavity search. They appear ignorantly blissful, not realizing that when they finally reach the TSA agent's control that all their personal belongings might be removed from their bags and strewn around the area for the disgustingly curious to see and for sticky-fingered thieves to assess. That kind of waiting I can do without.

Or how about the unfortunate and frustrating standstills that many of us have driven up to on interstate highways? Isn't that some of the worst waiting we have to endure? We're driving along, getting somewhere at a high rate of speed, when all of a sudden the red brake lights come on ahead of us and remain illuminated, warning us that the world up there is coming to a stop. That's when the sinking feeling hits us, and we whisper a hopeless, "Oh, no! How long is this gonna take?" And you know it's really bad when you pull up behind the last car and the people who were total strangers prior to the standstill are out playing rummy on the hoods of their vehicles, cooking hamburgers on their tailgates, and exchanging addresses because friendships have developed. That's not good waiting either.

And there is nothing pleasant when sitting in a doctor's holding room. After tolerating the delay in the main lobby and dreading the possible probing, poking, and pinching that is inevitable, then having to sit alone in a smaller room for who knows how long and look at disgustingly ugly pictures of the insides of sick people—that's lousy waiting. (And to think we pay big bucks for the privilege too!) Then there's the lab test results. With all the technology available, why must we wait two weeks after a biopsy to find out if that lump is cancer? That's one I've yet to figure out. I'm sure some lab person will seek me out now to explain it to me, but whatever he or she says, it won't make the drawn-out, nail-biting vigil by the phone any more fun.

But there is a *good* kind of waiting. It's when there's something positive at the end. Thankfully, there's plenty of lines in which to linger that has better rewards—enough of them at least to balance out most of the bad waiting. One of my more memorable experiences in regard to voluntarily getting in a waiting line because of the thrill on the far end took place in Ohio around 1979.

I was in a band that was invited to perform during "Christian Day" at King's Island near Cincinnati. We arrived plenty early in the day because part of the benefit for the band members was a free pass to the amusement park. I was especially excited because I knew about...The Beast.

Back then I was a roller coaster junkie, and The Beast was one of the most famous rides of the times. For a full six minutes or so a person could enjoy a neck-popping, vocal cord-stripping, hip-bruising ride on a state-of-the-art machine that boasted some of the highest peaks and lowest valleys known to those who thirsted for a violent, near-death experience. But to enjoy those six precious minutes the riders had to stand in a line that resembled the winding path bowels take through the human abdomen.

Packed with people bunched together tightly and moving slower than a snail with a limp, the line snaked around the parallel metal pipes for what seemed hundreds of yards. It's the kind of line that allows people to pass each other over and over—so many times that faces are memorized down to the moles and stray hairs, T-shirt messages become absolute truth, and conversations overheard come in bits and pieces, some being so interesting (or appalling) that it is hard to wait until you get close enough to hear again.

For a good 40-plus minutes I shuffled through that line. And I did it six times that day! Why? Because there was something on the other end of it that I found exhilarating. It was something I wanted, a challenge I dreamed about. And once I did it the first time and the ride lived up to the expectations I had placed on it, I couldn't get enough. I was finally forced to leave The Beast because there was a concert to do.

To balance out the other waits in life that are not so enjoyable, there are more places besides amusement parks where waiting has its sweet spoils. On the high-end of life there are glorious places like maternity waiting rooms, where family members excitedly anticipate the announcement that a new little one has arrived. I went to one of those rooms as a first-time grandfather not too long ago. That was some really great waiting! (Her name is Lily Anne, by the way, the latest fawn in the Chapman herd.)

In the everyday category of places where waiting can be enjoyable are locations such as movie theaters, concert halls, NASCAR events, a favorite restaurant, and check-out counters at Bass Pro or Cabelas. The lines at these places are not at all toilsome. I gladly bear them because of what I expect to find in the distance. But of all the places that involve waiting, the deer stand is definitely my favorite.

I can confidently say that as far as I'm concerned sitting alone on a deer stand has not once felt like drudgery. Even when I head home empty-handed I still feel refreshed for having been out there. This view of how pleasurable even a shot-less hunt can be reminds me of what the granddad of the late singer Harry Chapin said to his grandson. He said something to the effect of

> "Harry, there's two kinds of tired. There's a bad tired
> and a good tired. When you come to the end of the day
> exhausted because you've labored throughout all of it

in order to help someone else fulfill their dreams, that's a bad tired. But when your day ends and the hard work you did was for the sake of your own dream, even if you didn't make any money, that's a good tired.

Good deer-stand waiting, like a good tired, means that even if the critters don't show up there is always something about it that makes the waiting worth the effort. One reason most hunters agree this is true is because going hunting is something we *want* to do. And just because we might go home with an unpunched tag doesn't mean we're leaving the woods empty-handed. There have been times when I've left the stand with the memory of a sunrise that genuinely melted my emotions, a sight so lovely that I was reminded to say a quiet "thank You!" to the Creator. Is that a trophy? You bet!

On more than one occasion I have unloaded my bow or gun and headed to the truck with the refreshment of a few hours of blessed solitude. During these valuable breaks from the rest of the world I am often able to concentrate on praying for those I love. Or I get to go through some things I need to think about. Is that a good use of time? Yes, Sir!

If you and I redeem the time on a hunt in this way, we're doing the kind of waiting mentioned in the Old Testament book of Psalms: "Wait for the LORD; be strong and let your heart take courage; yes, wait for the LORD" (27:14). On the surface this passage seems to imply that when it comes to waiting for God, all we need to do is find a park bench and sit there quietly with folded hands and sooner or later He will come strolling by. That is not the meaning at all. To *wait* in this verse has a proactive meaning. The original word (*qavah*) means to "bind together by twisting." Essentially, those of us who effectively wait for God will redeem the time by "wrapping ourselves around" Him. To get that tightly intertwined with God requires a very active approach to a relationship with Him. Conversing with Him in prayer, listening to Him through His Word, studying and worshiping Him, allowing Him to influence every aspect of our lives is good waiting.

Deer hunters, for the most part, don't have a problem grasping this scriptural insight. We rarely sit on a deer stand thoughtless and brain dead. We "wrap ourselves around the hunt" by constantly watching the woods, carefully looking for the slightest movement. We mentally rehearse our shooting methods, and we take note of weather and wind. Our minds are busy. This active approach creates pure excitement from the first moment of a hunt to the last. And, more importantly, it tutors us about how to wait on the Lord. What a deal!

While there are some unquestionably wonderful by-products of keeping a vigil on a deer stand, such as learning how and why to redeem the time, seeing deer is the ultimate reason I gladly linger there. The anticipation of sighting the subtle movement of brownish-colored fur amid the thicket or catching the flicker of a white-tipped tail in the distance— pure heaven. And it's this unique aspect of deer hunting that has taught me more about how to enjoy the rest of life than nearly anything else.

Life is very similar to a deer hunt. It's a wait. The question to ask is, What will be the reward of my waiting? Whatever that expectation is will dictate whether or not my waiting is bad or good. If I believe the wait will yield something dreadful or even nothing at all, then life will surely be void of true joy. However, if I expect the wait to result in something wonderful—something even better than a huge trophy buck—then the sweetness of anticipation makes life much more enjoyable.

I will be forever grateful that I have something wonderful to look forward to as I wait on the "deer stand" of this life. The very thought of the divine sighting that I fully expect makes living feel like one uninterrupted day in the hunter's woods, where every moment is filled with the hope of seeing the prize I search for!

> Behold what manner of love the Father has bestowed on us, that we should be called children of God! Therefore the world does not know us, because it did not know Him. Beloved, now we are children of God; and it has not yet been revealed what we shall be, but we know that when He is revealed, we shall be like Him, *for we shall see Him as He is.* And everyone who has this hope in Him purifies himself, just as He is pure (1 John 3:1-3 NKJV).

> For the grace of God that brings salvation has appeared to all men, teaching us that, denying ungodliness and worldly lusts, we should live soberly, righteously, and godly in the present age, looking for the blessed hope and glorious appearing of our great God and Savior Jesus Christ, who gave Himself for us, that He might redeem us (Titus 2:11-14 NKJV).

If these passages describe your expectations as they do mine; then, my friend, we are enjoying some really great waiting!

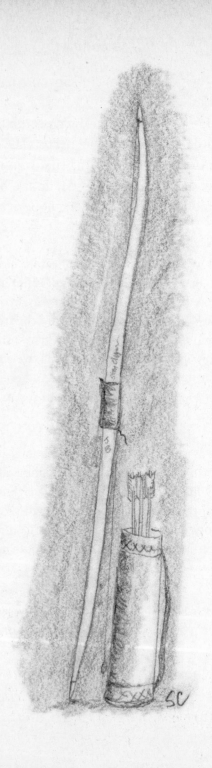

2

Crooked Bows

I don't remember exactly what I was doing in the yard that early summer day when I saw the square brown delivery truck coming down our driveway. However, I'll never forget what the driver put in my hands. As he headed back toward the paved road I stood in my yard holding a long, sturdy, cardboard tube that was addressed to me. I wondered what on earth it was.

I headed into the house to get a knife so I could open up the package to see what came. As I ripped the tape off the top to get to the prize inside I felt like I did when I was a youngster tearing into a box of Cracker Jacks. I was excited! The packing tightly filled the innards of the round container, and though it wasn't easy, I was finally able to pull the contents from it.

I couldn't believe what I was holding. It was a beautiful, handmade longbow. The return address showed that it had come all the way from Lone Pine, in the great state of Nebraska. When I read the note inside I realized the gift was from the skilled hands of a gentleman I had met there several months before named Joel Barrows. He shaped and finished the wood, made the string, boned the tips with deer antler, and even added a wind direction thread that was mounted to the black leather grip. It was, without question, one of the nicest gifts I have ever received. Knowing what a tremendous amount of time and effort it took to build such a thoughtful offering, I was humbled to be holding it in my hands.

Almost before the brown truck could drive out of sight I strung the bow and ran to get my collection of cedar arrows and a protective finger tab out of the garage. I keep a shooting block target in my backyard, and in about the time it takes a buck to turn and run once it "winds" a feller, I was coming to full draw with the longbow.

Not being a frequent user of the traditional style archery equipment I started up close to the target, at about five yards. That distance might sound easy to some folks, but a 15-foot shot with a bow that requires the archer to depend only on God-given instincts to hit the intended target makes a 2½' x 2' foam block seem like shooting at a match box. Furthermore, I didn't want to miss because there is no fun in crawling around in the yard on all fours while gingerly patting the grass with the palm of my hand. That's the process I use to feel for that slight hump that indicates there might be an unintentionally misplaced arrow that has slid just under the surface of the lawn. Seeing me crawl around is a sight I'm sure makes the neighbors wonder about my sanity! So I was compelled to make each shot connect with the block.

I have to admit, though I may never win contests at traditional archery competitions, I do think I have a pretty good feel for shooting instinctively. With surprising consistency I was grouping the arrows in a respectable area about the size of a dinner plate…at five yards. So I braved up a little and backed the distance to about ten yards and then about fifteen. That decision made it necessary to pat the yard a couple of times, but thankfully after shooting for a while I managed to still have the same number of shafts I started with.

About 20 minutes into enjoying the new addition to my archery arsenal, I took a rest to give my shoulders a break and to admire the wooden work of art in my hands. As I looked closely at it from tip to tip I discovered something I failed to see when I looked it over after it first arrived. In my excitement I didn't notice that it had my name on it! Joel had not only scribed his own sign in the bow; he had also personalized it for me near the grip. What a true treasure!

I shot a little more that day and grew increasingly impressed with how smooth the release of the string felt, how quiet it was, and how natural the feel was in my hands. The 50 pounds of pull was not overly taxing on my aging joints. In regard to finishing with my quiver still full, I will admit that the second session of shooting resulted in one cedar seed being permanently sown somewhere. The only consolation is that maybe someday I'll step outside and find an arrow tree growing near the house. And when the tree is fully mature it will yield wooden shafts that will be fletched with feathers, preknocked, field-tipped, and fully crested with orange and white (in honor of the Tennessee Volunteers!). Annie will be grateful that I'll never have to dip into our coffers for another dozen arrows.

As I was putting my "Barrows longbow" away in its shipping box to be safely stored until I used it again, an interesting feature caught my eye. I was quite surprised that I had not already seen it. The bow was barely down into the tube when

I noticed that it was not exactly straight. At first I wondered if it was my imagination so I pulled it out and checked it over closely. When I took it by the grip and held it out from my body as far as I could I said out loud, "Yep, this bow is sure enough crooked."

I couldn't believe my eyes. After just experiencing about 30 or 40 minutes of smooth releases, nicely flying arrows, and happily a lot of good hits on the foam block, I realized that all along I was using a crooked stick. I thought, "No way should this bow be yielding such precision."

I was absolutely amazed. My compound bow that has a high-tech aluminum riser made with a computer-generated machining device, perfectly matched fiberglass limbs, and wheels and cables that have been scientifically engineered for utmost operational consistency didn't feel any sweeter than the Barrows bow. I realized that even though there is an incredible span of time that separates the discovery of the technology that goes into the building of each type of bow, the two were nearly identical in terms of their potential accuracy. I tucked that discovery away in the file cabinet of my brain that is marked "There's gotta be a lesson in this somewhere."

As the days passed I couldn't help but string up the longbow and poke more holes in the foam block in the back-yard. It was more fun than a fellow should be allowed to have while outdoors. Though I used it often and would occasionally note its wandering shape, the fact that the bow was crooked didn't yield an insight until one Saturday afternoon later that summer. It happened while I sat in a sound booth at a church listening to my wife deliver the keynote address at a women's conference. She was teaching about the life of Abraham from the Old Testament.

Annie told the group of women, "Without question, Abraham, or Abram as he was known when we first meet him in the later portion of Genesis 11, is considered one of the great patriarchs of our faith. However, he was not a perfect man." Using a metaphor that the ladies would understand, Annie continued, "He did some things that require us to view him through a 'soft lens' in order to see him as God saw him. To explain, the 'soft lens' was a movie camera attachment first used many years ago in the movie making industry before computer technology replaced it. The soft lens gave the picture a slightly blurred effect. While the purpose of the lens may have been to generate a certain emotion in the movie viewer, it also did something for the beauty-conscious actresses of the day that some of them probably demanded. On a close-up shot, a soft lens would practically erase all wrinkles and other imperfections on their faces."

Moving on, Annie further explained, "In spite of his flaws, Abraham was viewed by God through the 'soft lens of grace.' Because God had tested him by directing him to pack up and leave the pagan culture of his homeland, and the fact that Abraham obeyed the call, God considered him to be a man whose heart was true and willing to be obedient. However, Abraham's actions didn't always show it.

"Most of us know, for example, two of the notable blunders he made. One, because he feared that the Egyptians would kill him in order to take his beautiful wife, Sarah, he asked her to tell a lie for him and say to the Egyptians that she was his sister. This scheme involved a half-truth since Sarah was his half-sister. Yet a half-truth is a whole lie. Abraham's plan did prolong his life, and he was treated well by the Pharaoh. That is, until the king and his house were struck with plagues because of Sarah. As a result, Abraham and his wife, along with all that he owned, were thrown out of Egypt. They were fortunate not to be killed. But God spared them because He had a plan for their lives."

Annie continued, "A second familiar mistake Abraham made is found in Genesis 16. It involved the impatience he showed regarding God's promise to make of him a great nation. He knew that in order for this to happen Sarah needed to bear him a son to propagate his lineage. Sarah, however, was beyond the childbearing years and unable to provide a son. Taking matters into her own hands, she talked Abraham into having a child with her maid, Hagar. Her weak and impatient husband decided to listen to the manipulations of his wife, and the result was Ishmael, a son, a boy who became a wild man who eventually became the father of the Arab tribes, Israel's fiercest enemy to this day. This is proof that God's way is the best way, but Abraham fell short of embracing it. Yet God kept His promise, and in time Isaac came along."

As I continued to listen to Annie tell about Abraham's human imperfections, I was amazed, along with the ladies who listened, that God would have ever chosen to use such a man. Yet what Annie said next really captured my attention as well as my imagination.

"Abraham's flesh may have been a little bit bent, but his heart was straight!"

As you can probably imagine, my mind left the building and raced a few states away to the room in my house in Tennessee where the Barrows bow was stored. I quietly rejoiced as I whispered, "Wow…God shoots straight with crooked bows!"

What an incredible picture. Even the great patriarch of

our faith had a history that didn't line up with perfection. Yet the arrows of God's truth flew accurately from his life. How could this be? The answer to that question can be found in Joel Barrow's workshop.

Skilled bowyers, especially those like Joel who work with Osage orange wood, the kind he used to make the bow he sent to me, will agree that a perfect bow never begins with a perfect stick of wood. The fact is, there is no such thing as a flawless stave from which a bowyer begins the process. Instead, the key to a great shooting bow is in the amount of understanding the bowyer has of the wood and the level of his or her ability to work with it.

The same can be said of people. Romans 3, verses 9 and 23, is an assessment of the quality of each of us as spiritual staves: "There is none righteous, not even one" and "for all have sinned and fall short of the glory of God." Except for Christ Jesus, there has not been a perfect example of humanity since Adam and Eve transgressed in the Garden of Eden. Once sin entered the world all who have been born begin from day one to grow like Osage orange wood—twisted, crooked, full of knots, hard to the core, and hard to work with. Even the most notable among us are flawed in one way or another. Consider, for example, the following short list of other well-known names from the Bible who had crooked turns connected to their reputations.

> Moses—a murdered Egyptian
> Jeremiah—harsh personality
> The psalmist David—Bathsheba
> The apostle Peter—the crowing rooster
> The apostle Paul—persecuted Christians

While I certainly don't revel in the flaws of these famous saints of the Bible, the fact that God saw potential in them, even with their imperfections, is most encouraging. I feel this way because I too cannot boast of a life without knots and twists. God's determination to use us is not thwarted by our flaws! He is fully capable and willing to work around them. He certainly made something useful out of the individuals from the Bible whom I just mentioned. Look at the list again...

Moses—the exodus leader
Jeremiah—the heartbroken prophet
David—king over all of Israel
Peter—early church leader
Paul—apostle, missionary, teacher

The records show that these folks from the Scriptures, along with Abraham, have at least one thing in common. They were imperfect people who became perfect examples of the Master Bowyer's willingness to choose and use flawed individuals. Thankfully, the human demonstrations of His willingness to use crooked bows are not confined to people found in the pages of the Bible. There are living and breathing examples among us in our times. And interesting enough, I learned about one of these individuals as a result of another gift that was delivered one day to my home. The Barrows Longbow came by truck but I found this unforgettable treasure in my mailbox.

The sender was a gentleman named Kenny Johnson. Inside his package were two cassette tapes. One was the delightful and moving music of Kenny and his wife, Donna. The other tape was his personal testimony. As I listened to him speaking on the cassette, I was struck with the sincerity in

Kenny's voice as he shared the story of his life journey and how he became a writer of gospel songs.

From the recording I learned that just three months before he was born his dad abandoned his mother and their house full of kids. Amazingly, on the very day of Kenny's birth, his brother, the eldest of nine children, became a Christian and shortly thereafter began taking his mother and his siblings to church. Eventually, Eva Lee Posey Johnson (his mother's full name), found the source of her strength to be rooted in her faith in Jesus, and she became a mother who was determined to raise her children in the admonition of the Lord.

That faith would be tested sorely through the years by the haunting sorrow of an absent husband and father, as well as the daunting challenge of providing food and shelter for her kids. Perhaps one of the toughest moments for Eva Lee came the day she heard that one of her sons had been killed while serving his country in the U.S. Army. Yet her resolve didn't wane, and she held the family together. Today, as Kenny puts it, she watches all of her remaining children from the "balcony of heaven" as they continue on and lead full and healthy lives.

Needless to say, when the tape was finished I was melted butter. But of all that I heard, I remember being especially moved by a specific part of Kenny's story that involved a handmade item his mother had crafted. I was so moved in fact that I documented this particular part of his account in a song lyric.

The Pocket

Daddy left in January
And I was born in April
I was down the line, the last of nine

And I'll be forever grateful
For the way that Mama stayed with us
And said our names to Jesus
Oh, but she was sad
She missed our dad
And wondered why he'd ever leave us

We didn't have a dime
But we were rich
And Mom was good at sewing
She took a bag of old cut-up rags
And before it started snowing
She made a quilt to keep us warm
And I slept underneath it
But in the seams was dad's old blue jeans
Among all the other pieces

Then one night I'll not forget
In that quilt I found a pocket
I remember what my Mama said
When I put my hand inside it
She said, "The night your daddy said goodbye
He left everything behind him
Now where your hand is
He once had his."
She left the room crying

How many nights I cried myself to sleep
Underneath that cover
With my hand where his had been
Back when he loved our mother
But sometimes that memory floods my soul
If I tried I couldn't stop it
Now that old quilt is gone
But I live on

With my hand inside that pocket
Yes, my daddy's gone
But I live on
With my hand inside that pocket[1]

Today, Kenny and his wife, Donna, have devoted their lives as musicians and singers to encourage others to put their faith in the Lord. Kenny writes all of their songs, and the quality and effectiveness of his lyrics are proof of at least two undeniable facts. One, his ministry through music is evidence that his mother was richly rewarded for her resolve to pass the legacy of trusting God's grace and mercy down to her children. It is an honor she definitely deserves.

The other fact confirmed by Kenny's life is that God truly is willing and able to use imperfect people to accomplish His perfect will. That truth could be clearly heard in a most memorable statement that was made on the cassette he sent to me, and it is especially relevant to the picture found in the Barrows longbow. Kenny humbly said, "My dad being gone may have left me a little warped, but I'm not weird. The Lord still uses me, and I'm truly grateful for it."

The following is a portion of one of Kenny's lyrics. It is more proof that God really does shoot straight with crooked bows!

Playing Baseball with Jesus

Jesus doesn't count the strikes
He just lets me swing away
For surely He knew there would come a time
I would be too broken to pray
He pitches the ball with nail-scarred hands
Over and over again
He doesn't want to see me lose
He wants to see me win

Another Look at Life from a Deer Stand

At the crack of the bat
I head for the base
Trying to score a run
But I'm a big boy now
And life's game is not always fun

Then comes the words, "Batter up!"
Booming from the Throne
And I just smile when I realize
God's not trying to get me out
He's just trying to get me home[2]

3

Deer Already in the Heart

One thing you can definitely expect while deer hunting is the unexpected. This story is proof:

I sat staring straight ahead for several minutes feeling very puzzled about why I hadn't seen even one deer that evening. The field of nearly mature soybeans usually hosted several whitetails. In my estimation I should have had at least one sighting with the hour being so close to twilight. Instead the search had been a bust. But as I was about to give up, the familiar sight of a light-brown color against a background of dark-green crop caught my eye. It often happens that way. Just when I think all the whitetails have packed up and moved to another county leaving me to have to sell my house and move there to be near them, something happens to make me want to stay put.

I moved my head to the left and fixed my gaze on one of the nicest bucks I had sighted all year. Standing near him were a couple of sizable does, two younger females, and possibly a button buck. Their heads bobbed up and down as they fed and cautiously surveyed the ten-acre field they had entered. They had no idea that I was not too far away watching and wishing.

The wind would not let up as it came across my left shoulder. The noise it created, however, served to cover the audible reaction I involuntarily gave to finally seeing fur. "This is what I've been waiting for! One, two, three, four, five...and one of them is definitely a taker!"

I quietly mumbled my feelings of elation as I ended my count and quick assessment of the biggest member of the group. Only serious hunters know how thrilling even a distant sighting can be, especially when it has been a while since the eyes have had a feast on the beast we so love to pursue. It can make us do strange things like...well...talk to ourselves. It's scary.

The small herd was feeding at the edge of the field. They were likely waiting for the safety of darkness before moving out farther. I continued to look each deer over and tried to memorize the shooter's rack. Even though he was about 300 yards away, I could see that he had plenty of height. I guessed that there were probably at least eight points. I didn't take my eyes off him as I rehearsed a shot.

I knew if I was going to take a shot that the crosshairs would have to be about three or four inches directly above the buck's "boiler room." The broadside stance he had taken as he munched on the soybeans was ideal for effective placement. I couldn't have asked for a better opportunity. Then it happened...BAM!

All I remember to this day was the sound of the air bag exploding in my face, engulfing my body and not allowing me to become a projectile of flesh and bone against the steering column. The crushing sound of the front end of my nearly new four-wheel drive, full-size pickup was momentarily lost in the earsplitting report of the inflatable safety device.

As I quickly pushed the deflating "party balloon" away from my stunned body, I was amazed at how quiet my world had quickly become. Then in a few seconds the screeching noise of stopping traffic and the concerned passersby running toward my truck, as well as a hissing sound that came from under my hood, alerted me that "maybe" I hadn't seen the slowing traffic and "maybe" I was sitting at the wheel of a truck that had just rear-ended someone's vehicle. Unfortunately, I was right on both counts.

As it turned out, neither I nor the poor fellow who had fallen victim to my incessant desire to see whitetails were seriously injured. Thankfully we suffered only a few scratches and some muscle strains. However, my pickup and my wallet took a real beating as a result of the collision.

Adding to the pain were the bruises that my ego had to endure because it didn't take long for the jokes to start. Of course their digs were my own fault. I made the mistake of admitting that my accident was the product of liking to drive to and from work on routes where I could enjoy some sightings. Once that news got around, I had to put up with statements like, "You better hold on for 'deer' life if you're gonna ride to work with him!" or "Hey, Man, do you need a designated hunter to take you home?" I decided that if I couldn't lick 'em, I'd join 'em. So I had a license plate made that warns, 'Honk if I'm huntin.' The problem is, I was serious!

What a blessing that this "highway hunter" lived to laugh about his sobering close call. I am quite sure that if others of us were as candid, we would confess the same dangerous tendency to engage in the hunt while driving. I am sure this mistake is more widespread among hunters than we care to admit because simply, I've done the same thing. The only difference between us is the shape of the front bumpers on our vehicles. Thankfully, I don't have any damaging evidence so far that I can be just as preoccupied while cruising along a farm-lined highway.

Though the accident was regrettable for both parties, there is something redeemable among the carnage. Specifically, there is a picture in the scenario that can provide helpful guidance to those who would like to avoid another kind of self-inflicted disaster. It has to do with the striking resemblance between what the hunter struggled with that caused his roadway blunder and what men wrestle with who are mentioned in Matthew 5:28. The passage reveals a mistake that can result in a wreck that can cause even more damage on the highway of life.

In verse 27, Jesus is speaking. He says, "You have heard that it was said, 'You shall not commit adultery...'" Then in the next verse He warns, "but I say to you that everyone who looks at a woman with lust for her has already committed adultery with her in his heart." (Note: The word, "look" in the original language of the Bible does not refer to an unexpected glance, but a deliberate gaze or lingering stare.)

The similarity between the highway hunter's error and the adulterer's mistake is in the words "in his heart." For the longest time I had it all backward when it came to understanding the process involved in committing adultery as described in the passage. I assumed that looking at a woman led to the sin of lusting after her. It was a misconception that I held to until the unforgettable moment I gleaned some wisdom from a wise Bible teacher. Essentially, he said, "Look at the passage closely. Can't you see that looking at a woman does not lead to adultery? Instead, it is the adultery that is *already in the heart* that leads to lustfully looking at her. The looking is telling you that you are already in trouble!"

That revelation transformed the way I think about facing the temptation to commit adultery, whether the enticement would be in the reality of the flesh or in the secret recesses of my heart. Like the red light on my truck dash that alerts me that something is wrong inside the engine, I now realize that the temptation to extend a stare at a woman is a warning sign telling me that something deadly is lurking within.

Back to the highway hunter, there is a good reason that the rear bumper of another person's vehicle is the only thing he tagged that evening. It was because he was distracted from his duties as an attentive driver. But what made him so prone to look away? What made his eyes willingly linger on the deer instead of the road? By his own admission his intention to gaze at the whitetails was in place when he got behind the wheel. In other words, he had *deer already in his heart!* When he climbed into his truck and headed out of his workplace parking lot, he preplanned to take the rural route home. He knew well that the fields he would pass were favored by the wild things he wanted to see. The fact that the deer were there didn't necessarily surprise him. He was fully hoping to see the critters. He was looking because he planned to look.

Such is the case for far too many of us who make ourselves victims of the reckless act of premeditated adultery. Some guys, for example, use certain motels as they travel because they know there are "those channels" on the TV service the hotel uses. Other fellows might go to a particular restaurant because they know in advance that the waitresses there will be scantily clad. In an even more subtle scheme, some of us willingly take our families to the beach because we know, before we even get there, about the "sightings" that are available at the oceanside. And sunglasses are a must at a public beach for more reasons than bright sunshine. These, and the many other ways that men can make advance plans to feed their wandering eyes could be avoided if only the "red warning light of lust on the dash of their hearts" was heeded.

The convicting truth that lust is not a product of looking but looking is a product of lust was an insight I shared with my wife not long after I learned about it. And while the revelation was fresh on our minds, we both encountered a very vivid picture of what it meant.

It happened one day while we were riding together in our van. We had been in North Carolina for a weekend of presenting marriage seminars, and on the seven-hour drive back to our home in Tennessee we traded shifts at the wheel in order to avoid stopping to rest. Annie was driving, and we were around the midway point of our trip as we passed through the area where the exits to Gatlinburg, Tennessee, are located.

At that time I was actively looking for a replacement for my old motorcycle. Biking is something I sincerely enjoy, and I like it so much that I will sometimes go into dealerships just to gawk at the art that can be found in the "metal ponies." Needless to say, a motorcycle was already on my mind as we neared a particular stretch of I-40, where a Honda bike store is located. I knew it was there because I had seen it many times as we traveled to and from the east.

As Annie drove through the area she noticed I was intently staring to my left over the hood without looking away. My gaze continued for a couple of miles because I was determined not to miss even a glimpse of the bikes I assumed (and hoped) would be sitting outside the showroom in the April open air. I also was well aware that the shop was close enough to the highway that I could likely get a quick look at the particular model I favored if it was displayed.

When we went rolling by the dealership I didn't bat a

peeper as I gazed portside at the passing sight. I didn't even see Annie in my field of view when my eyes went from looking at the store through the front windshield to watching it disappear into the distance through the back windows of the van. All I saw were shiny pipes, shapely handlebars, sweeping fenders, bright aluminum wheels, sparkling windshields, and studded leather saddles. I was consumed by the glorious scene.

As I reluctantly turned my head back to the forward position Annie spoke up and said, "You have Hondultery in the heart!"

"What?" I said the word as innocently as I could to make my very perceptive wife believe I didn't know what she was talking about. But I knew exactly what she meant. She did too as she said it again, only this time with a tone of confidence that didn't allow me to weasel out of the truth.

"Yes, Sir, you had motorcycle already in the heart. That's why you stared at that Honda store like you did when we went by." Then she laughed understandably and said, "You need a napkin. You're drooling on your lap."

I was, without question, caught in the act of Hondultery, just as Annie observed. I could not deny it. As I nursed the slight sting of the comparison my dear wife had just made, she added a little more light to the insight of the picture we were seeing.

"Notice *I* didn't look at the Honda store. I would have never known it was there. Why?" She asked the question even though she already knew the answer, and so did I.

"I didn't look because I don't have motorcycles in my heart! On the other hand, had there been a Lenox Outlet Store…well…you know what I mean." Knowing her extreme interest in dishes, I did know what she meant, and the thought of it made my credit cards shudder!

On the surface, the Matthew 5:28 passage might appear to offer little hope to the man who struggles to avoid the spiritually dangerous act of allowing himself a lingering, lustful look at a woman. Yet there is another way to look at the picture in the text that will provide some encouragement in his determination to resist the temptation:

> If it's true that intentionally looking upon a woman is a sign that adultery is already present in the heart, then deliberately choosing *not* to look at her can be an indication that the man is actively in pursuit of righteousness.

In that moment when a man realizes he is faced with the temptation to extend an ungodly stare at a woman, if he instead chooses to look away from her, it can be a sign that he is being motivated by the worthy pursuit of holiness. When this is the case, righteousness is the victor in his life. And the triumph he experiences with controlling his eyes can be directly contributed to his understanding that the battle began not in his eyes, but in his spirit.

Until I understood the real truth in Matthew 5:28, I errantly told men that if they could stop adultery at the gate of their eyes, the sin would not find its way to their hearts. As commendable as this idea may be, the reality is, if a man can keep adultery out of his heart, the sin will not find its way to his eyes. Ultimately, what the eyes of flesh see is not the real problem. Instead, it is what can be visualized by the eyes of the inner man that causes the struggle. This truth is revealed in Matthew 5:29, immediately following the passage about adultery. In this verse Jesus says, "If your right eye makes you stumble, tear it out and throw it from you; for it is better for you to lose one of the parts of your body, than for your whole body to be thrown into hell."

The key word in this passage is *if*. The implication is that if the eye were the problem, the solution would be very easy. Just pluck it out. If the hand were a thief's problem, the answer would be simple as well. However, the first and greatest challenge for a man is not in controlling what his eyes see on the outside. No, the ultimate task is monitoring what he allows himself to think about on the inside.

Thankfully, there are men whom I personally know who understand that the battle for moral purity starts in the heart. These men have been living examples of how to successfully fight and win. One of them is my own father, Paul J. Chapman. In all of my growing up years I never saw him look at women in a lustful way. Also I never heard him use unwholesome verbiage about another woman. His example of how "heart control" can help a person be in command of his eyes is at the top of my list of those who have inspired me to a higher standard.

My son, Nathan, has also been an encouragement to me. While I have no doubt whatsoever that he is most appreciative of the marvelous creation of the woman (and he comes by it naturally!), I am grateful to report that he has displayed only an abiding respect for them. Today Nathan is married, and his wife, Stephanie, is the main benefactor of his ongoing determination to show reverence to God's warning about inward lust.

Another person who greatly appreciates Nathan's resolve to guard against the sin of inner adultery is his father-in-law, Ed. What valuable comfort Nathan offers to a man who deeply loves the young lady he carefully raised in the admonition of the Lord. Gratefully, I have known that same delight as a father-in-law.

My son-in-law, Emmitt Beall, has also provided a great deal of joy in regard to honoring our daughter with the fight against the enemy of lust. Actually, I noticed it early on in their relationship. When he was dating Heidi, I distinctly remember the elation I felt one Sunday afternoon while we were all watching a football game. The Dallas Cowboys were playing, and when that particular football team name comes up, a lot of American men immediately connect it to the Dallas Cowboy cheerleaders.

As the game progressed, the lead widened and the interest of the broadcast directors switched from the action on the playing field to the cheerleaders who were prancing on the sidelines. Consequently the cameras would cut away to them quite frequently. I noticed that each time the TV screen filled with bouncing flesh, Emmitt would look across the room either at someone else or at a picture on the wall and even, at times, he'd look up at the ceiling fan. That day I became his biggest fan. I was not only totally impressed with the punches he was swinging at the foe of lustful thoughts, I couldn't wait for a guy like him to be a part of our family. I knew my daughter's life would be better because of Emmitt's willingness to stand on the front lines of the war and do battle with the enemy of adultery.

I am extremely grateful to have men in my circle of family and friends who inspire me to a higher moral standard with their determined pursuit of godliness. I want to be like them and return the inspiration. They are the kind of valuable acquaintances mentioned in the latter part of 2 Timothy 2:22: "Now flee from youthful lusts and pursue righteousness, faith, love and peace, *with those who call on the Lord from a pure heart.*" How incredibly crucial these type of comrades can be to one another! But their worth goes beyond helping each other be successful at winning over temptation. Not only can we motivate each other to the spiritually noble goal of living in purity, we can also lift each other up in times of failure. And, as most of us will readily admit, failure will happen.

I offer the following lyric to encourage you if you are dealing with the nagging feelings of guilt that spiritual and moral failure can foster in a human heart. I hope God's fathomless grace will help you get back up and keep pressing on in your pursuit of righteousness.

The Mark

He's the aim of my affection
The One I want to please
The target of petitions
When I'm on my knees

I can point to none more worthy
Of my devoted heart
Yet He's the One who shows me mercy
When I miss the mark

Lord help me keep your holiness
Always in my sights
And the arrows of allegiance
Straight and true in flight

To the center of Your will
Father guide my heart
And I'll thank You for Your mercy
When I miss the mark[1]

4

Deer Don't Talk

A friend of mine forwarded this email to me:

A married couple was having some trouble in their relationship, and out of desperation they went to see a counselor. They had not been in the office but a few minutes when the wife went into a tirade about how unloved and neglected she had felt in their 15 years of marriage. The counselor put his hand up as if to motion her to stop talking, got up from his chair, walked around the desk, and asked the wife to stand. Then he took her into his arms and proceeded to plant a very passionate, lingering kiss on her lips. When he was finished the woman just melted into her chair, obviously stunned but secretly flattered by what had just happened.

"Sir," the counselor addressed the surprised husband, "this is what your wife needs at least three times a week. Are you willing to commit to it?"

The husband leaned up in his chair and said to the counselor, "Yes, Sir. I can bring her in on Mondays and Wednesdays, but I usually go huntin' on Fridays so she'll have to find her own way here."

I have no idea where that story originated, but it's one of

my all-time favorites. Perhaps the reason it has jumped to my Top 20 list of great jokes is because of the gentle way that it humorously reminds me of one of my greatest struggles. Of all the things that I preach as an outdoorsman, perhaps the one thing that is most difficult for me to both preach and practice is maintaining a thoughtful sensitivity to my wife's feelings about my passion for hunting. In the book *A Hunter Sets His Sights,* I devoted a whole chapter to how much I appreciate my sweetheart. Entitled *Love Song of the Hunter,* it centered around a song that was written while on the deer stand of my affection for Annie.

More recently I completed a book to help men maintain a good balance between their marriages and their hobbies. It is called *The Good Husband's Guide to Balancing Hobbies and Marriage.* With all the insights I have espoused and have diligently tried to follow, the struggle remains intense in my heart to make sure Annie knows that I don't want my serious like of hunting to negatively affect my love for her. Though it is still a very real challenge at times to keep putting her first, I think I have proven that it remains my chief goal as a husband. And one of the very best indicators that I am doing a few things right is found in her smile.

Thankfully, my sweet wife has somehow managed to see a bit of humor in my ever-growing passion for grocery shopping from a tree perch. Her laughter tells me her feelings for me and for the hunt have not been wounded by me or my doing it. It really is a relief to see her grin and hear her chuckle from time to time about it. One of those times happened not too many seasons ago.

Both of our children were married, and when Thanksgiving came that year the six of us got together on the Tuesday before the usual Thursday holiday. The plan was to celebrate with a meal at our house so Nathan and Heidi and their spouses could travel to be with their in-laws on the actual holiday. Their departure would be around noon on Wednesday. That meant Annie and I would be alone on the eve of Thanksgiving Day, as well as on the actual holiday that would follow.

When Wednesday evening came things were very quiet around the house. Both of us were feeling the sting of how time had so quickly silenced the sound of children in our home. We quietly moped around wondering how the house could be so empty so quickly. We dealt with our bewilderment in very different ways. Annie loves to read so she dove into a book. I like to write songs so I went to my little "cubbyhole" office, put a pad and pen on the desk, and plucked around on the guitar, waiting for the "big one" to come along (a hit song, that is). The "noise" I was making filled a void.

As I strummed, hummed, and doodled, I looked across the room at the mount of my son's very first buck that hangs on the wall. It's a nice Tennessee six point. I stared at it for a long time, remembering the day he tagged it. He was a mere teenager and the Marlin lever action .30-30 rifle he was carrying had served him well. I could still feel the emotions that coursed through our hearts that morning. It was as if not one minute had passed.

Then my mind went to the fields we had hunted just 48 hours earlier where he had added a nice doe to our freezer stash. And that's when it hit me. As though my brain was going down one set of tracks and someone threw the lever to shift me to another set, my thoughts went from the precious memories of bygone days to the immediate future. Imaginations of where I could be the next morning, Thanksgiving day, began to excite me to the core.

I stopped picking the strings, put the pencil down, set my guitar back on its stand, and headed downstairs to the den. On the way, I quickly rehearsed how I would ask my darling and lovable wife to concede to the idea of me being on a deer stand the next morning. Here's what I said…

"Uh…Babe. .uh…you know, it sure is quiet around here."

Annie pulled her glasses off her face and looked up over her book at me. I have no doubt she knew what was coming. She had heard that tone in my voice before. Yet she didn't interrupt and say, "Oh…sure, why don't you go hunting in the morning? It'll do you good—clear your head, relieve some stress, make you happy. It's fine with me."

No, she didn't do that. It was only a passing hope. Instead she stared at me with an expression that seemed to say, "I know what you want to ask, and I'm gonna let you do it just so I can watch you grovel."

I went through with my request even though it didn't come out pretty. It came out as one long, strung together sentence that said, "Sure was a good dinner today you look nice your hair is shiny your pants fit what are you reading what do you think about me going hunting for a couple of hours in the morning?"

I couldn't believe I sounded so boyish. Seriously, the words came out like I was a 13-year-old, snot-nosed kid asking a girl's dad if I could date his snot-nosed daughter. But it must have looked really cute to Annie because what I heard next nearly floored me.

She put her bookmark in the page she was reading and closed the cover. Then she looked past me through the empty house and said, "You know, we had a great time with the kids. Not one cross word came from any of us. What a blessing to have had such a peaceful time. Some folks had fighting with their feast and would have rather had a morsel in peace. But, Steve, we had both the feast and the fun. I'm so thankful for that blessing that I want you to top it off with a Thanksgiving morning deer hunt. I'll sleep in, and when you get home I'll have a breakfast ready that will top all you've had this year."

I'm not quite sure what I may have done right to have heard what I had just heard, but I was not about to question it! I did the right thing. I went over and gave my wife a tender hug, thanked her, and promised I wouldn't spend the entire day away from the house.

When daylight came the next morning I was sitting on the ground on a three-legged stool at the brushy edge of a huge field on a friend's farm. As I leaned my back against a young elm and patiently waited for the shooting light to come on, I thought of how grateful I felt. With my rifle resting in my lap the 20-degree temperature didn't faze me. I was warmed by the fact that I was outside hunting!

I had promised myself not to take a shot at a deer unless it was heavy. A mature doe or a large antlered buck would be my limit. My unspoken hope was to see the ten-point that had shown himself only a couple of times during bow season.

The brilliant sun rays that came from behind me were golden as they washed across the open field where I sat. I almost broke out in a song of rejoicing at how incredibly beautiful the morning was. I was so thrilled with the sight and with being able to be there to enjoy it that I remember thinking how very fine it would be if I didn't even see an animal. The sunrise was a trophy in itself. But then I caught a glimpse of the tips of antlers.

There was a depression in the field about a hundred yards out. In it was a buck that was coming my way, but I wasn't yet sure of its size. My heart leaped with excitement, and I carefully put the .270 rifle to my shoulder and rested my elbows on my knees. Finally the deer came up the rise and stopped in full view. My nerves calmed when I realized that the deer was a juvenile, probably a year-and-a-half to a two-year-old male. His little nontypical five-point rack was adorable, but he was not a takeable deer today. I whispered to him, "You get to walk, little fellow." Then he did walk, and what I saw when he took a few steps made the pity meter peg to the far right.

His labored gate immediately revealed that he had been seriously wounded, possibly the afternoon or evening before. Through the scope I could see an open wound in his hind quarter. He took about eight or ten steps to the left and stopped broadside to me, panting as he stood there. I knew what had to be done, and my heart broke as I did it.

When the report of the .270 faded and silence returned to the area where I was, the young buck lay lifeless in the field. I gathered up my gear, walked out to him, grabbed one side of his small rack and drug him back to where I had been sitting. There I removed my plastic gloves and sharp knife out of my pack and prepared his carcass for the trip home.

After completing the field dressing I cleaned my hands and headed to my pickup truck. On the way I took out my cell phone and dialed my number at home. Annie answered and from the caller ID she knew it was me.

"Hey, Babe. Are you finished already?"

"Uh huh."

"Did you get something?"

"Uh…uh huh."

Annie could tell something wasn't right. "What's going on? Sounds like you're a little tentative."

I searched for the right words. "Well…I did get a deer, but I didn't want to do it."

"Explain."

"This deer, a young one, came across the field. I noticed that it had a really bad limp. I had promised myself not to shoot anything as young as he was, but it was a matter of mercy. I put him out of his misery. I hated to do it, but anyway, it's done."

Annie consoled me. "I know you wouldn't have shot the poor thing if you didn't think it was necessary. You did the right thing. Are you coming straight home or are you taking him on to Grissom's Meats first?"

"I'll come on home. It's cold enough that I can wait until tomorrow to take him to Grissom's. I'll be home in about 45 minutes."

Then Annie said, "Steve?"

The tone of her question made me wonder what she was about to say. The long pause between my name and the next words worried me a bit. But then she spoke again.

"I'm quite concerned about something."

"What's that?" I asked, hoping and praying she had not had a change of heart about my whereabouts that morning.

"Did you say the deer was limping badly and that's why you ended its life?"

"Yes."

"Do you remember last night when we went to bed and I mentioned how my varicose veins were acting up?"

"I sure do, Babe," I answered as lovingly as I could, hoping to win some husband points.

"Well, it's not much better this morning."

"Oh, I'm so sorry, Sweetheart."

"Don't be concerned with it. That problem will clear up. Something else concerns me."

Fearing that another medical emergency was arising, I swallowed hard and asked, "What should I be praying about?"

"Well, it concerns me that you are in such a benevolent mood this morning with your rifle."

"Really?" I asked.

She answered, "Yes. And that's why I'll try not to be limping around with this sore leg when you get home!"

Annie's quick wit brought the sunlight back to a morning for me that had started so gloriously but became clouded by the sad sight of an animal struggling in pain. I was thankful for the comic relief Annie provided.

There is one other story I like to tell that shows that Annie is not reserved about inserting humor into her tolerance of my passion for hunting. This true tale also involves a cell phone.

Since the onset of cellular technology I have committed to carrying a phone with me whenever I go to the woods. I do it for two good reasons. One, I like to assure Annie that I am safe and unharmed by occasionally checking in. She is aware that outdoorsmen, especially hunters, are not exempt from the inherent dangers related to their hobbies. I have scars on my left arm to make her point. The 18-foot, sudden and unexpected fall I took out of a tall, rough-barked tree left me with enough evidence to prove that hunting has its dangers. So, I have no problem with using the phone to make sure she knows I'm unharmed, especially if, for example I am tracking a bleeding deer into the dark hours of the evening.

Another reason I include a cell phone in my gear pack is that I enjoy calling Annie after I have met with success in the hunter's woods. I believe that for the most part the first person a husband/hunter wants to call with such good news is likely his best friend. For me that person is Annie. Whenever I recover a deer, I simply call and say something like, "Got a doe today!" If it's a buck I will briefly report, "Got a seven… or…got a six, a five, an eight, a nine," and so on. In all my years of hunting I had not yet downed a deer with points that numbered into the double digits, not until a most memorable recent season.

I'll never forget how excited I was after I arrowed a really huge buck, found it and dialed the number at home. With a little growl and a slightly braggadocio tone in my best manly voice, I said, "I'm standing over a 16, Babe."

The silence on the other end told me she was searching really hard for just the right accolades to offer her hero/husband/hunter. Then she broke the silence with,

"A 16? Would that be points or pounds?"

I was speechless as her words worked their way through my brain. Within milliseconds my mind that had been intoxicated with adrenalin was sobered with some of the best laughter I'd had in months. I couldn't believe what Annie had just said! I laughed so hard that the sniffles the cold morning had developed in my nose as I tracked the heavy beast sprayed liberally out onto my mustache. As I wiped the debris off my beard, I laughed even harder as I said to Annie, "Sure wish I could kiss you right now!"

Once again, there I was in the outdoors enjoying the thing

I like to do most, feeling totally at ease that my dear wife was completely accepting of where I was. Her laughter is a signal that tells me I am doing something right.

Along with Annie's wonderful wit that comforts me as a husband and hunter, there is another thing she does that tells me I'm doing well in my attempt to maintain her favor for my hobby. It comes in the form of two precious words that are valuable beyond measure.

Whenever I leave the house to head to the woods and Annie says, "Have fun!" then I know she has absolutely no problem with me leaving for a while. I can be totally free of guilt and absent of worry that I might be alienating her from the thing that provides so much enjoyment for me.

Not every husband I know enjoys that kind of freedom. There have been several guys I've spoken to who long to know that liberty, but it's just not happening. One fellow said about his marriage as it relates to his wife's struggle with his love of hunting, "It's been 12 years of marital bliss-ters!"

My dear brothers, or should I say "deer" brothers, if you are married I hope you are not only enjoying the thrill of hunting but, more importantly, I hope you are doing all you can to know the joy of a wife who happily supports you in it. I can personally report that it is a feat that is possible to accomplish. And your wife's smile can be one of the best sources of evidence that you're doing things right. If you're not seeing her smile, hearing her laughter, or hearing her say words similar to "Have fun!" I hope the following song lyric will inspire you to work harder at gaining...or regaining her favor.

Deer Don't Talk

There's a crowd down at the check-in station
Jimmy and his friends have gathered 'round
They're all looking at the one
He brought in this morning
It's a twelve and at least
Two hundred pounds

Jimmy said, "I wouldn't have got 'im
If I'd 've listened
To my wife
And what she said to me last night
She said, "I'm feelin' second place
In this whitetail chase."
Then they all laughed
When Jimmy said,
"And then she cried."

Then an old hunter standing round
Heard them talking
He stepped up and said,
"Looks like somebody found a prize.
But boys I hope you'll listen
To what I have to tell you."
Then he looked straight at Jimmy
In the eyes.

And he said, "Deer don't talk,
They don't say I love you
They don't reach out for you
When you're livin' all alone
And when your bed is cold
And you beg God just to hear her whisper
That's when it won't matter
What you're hangin' on the wall
'Cause deer don't talk."

Then Jimmy said, "Well I guess
I must be goin'
There's some things around the house
I gotta do."
And as he drove away
He looked into his mirror
And the old hunter waved
And smiled as if he knew

That he heard, "Deer don't talk
They don't say I love you
They don't reach out for you
When you're livin' all alone
And when your bed is cold
And you long just to hear her whisper
That's when it won't matter
What you're hangin' on the wall
'Cause deer don't talk."[1]

5

"Instandity"

I was nearly on a dead run going from my office to our product storage building, and then back to the office, to the mailing desk, to the email computer and whatever else that jumped up and screamed, "I need your undivided attention!" All the while I was checking my wristwatch to carefully monitor the time. I had to leave my driveway at 2:30 sharp because I had an important appointment…on a deer stand.

That morning while sitting in a ladder-type stand that was securely leaned against a huge oak at the edge of a soybean field I saw an unforgettable sight. And the mental image of what I saw munching on acorns had been chewing on my emotions since I got home at nine that morning. Across the field, perhaps 500 yards away I spotted a buck that I had not seen in the area up to that time. In my binoculars I could see that it sported possibly 10, maybe even 12 points on its very easily seen rack. Though it was so far away and not giving any sign of coming toward my position, the excitement still made me shake like I was riding on an old Harley-Davidson that was rumbling down the highway.

The thing that motivated me to hurry back to that field

when evening came was an assumption I made regarding the movement of the buck. According to where I first saw it and the direction it seemed to be heading, I made the leap that it had been feeding during the night in the soybeans and then worked its way into a patch of woods filled with acorns. When I caught sight of him he was feeding just at the edge of the woods and seemed to be going toward a thicket on the northern side of the farm. It was late September, and even though he was in the beginning stages of entering the rut season, I had a feeling his movements might still be somewhat predictable. So during my working hours I formulated my plan for where I would be that evening. Though it might have appeared that I was giving my office duties the full attention they needed, in my head I was making plans for an ambush.

I concluded that since the whitetails in our region were in a more calm time of their year, the big buck might leave his bungalow in the northside thicket and begin back-tracking to the soybean field somewhere around 5:45. His body size and rack dimensions told me he was old enough to know he should hang back in the shadows and wait until the cover of darkness to enter the open field. So my calculations put him in the acorns at about the time the sun was half to three quarters gone behind the hill. It would still be legal shooting light for me. And here's the kicker: I had a stand already hung in that grove of oaks that I was sure he would likely feed through. In fact, that morning I had considered getting into that spot but opted to hunt the opposite edge of the soybean field.

Why does it seem to always happen that when a fellow must leave for the woods at 2:30 in the afternoon an important call comes at 2:28? I nearly snapped my head off as I made every gesture I could think of to silently signal our office manager that I needed to go. Unfortunately, I couldn't get out of answering the call. However, I used the portable "walk-a-phone," and as I talked I multitasked and loaded my bow and backpack into my truck and started it to let it warm up. By 2:37 I was saying goodbye. By 2:39 I was backing out and on my way to enjoy a hunt that I considered one of the most promising I could remember for quite a while. I was pumped as I imagined what might happen.

Sunset would take place sometime after 6:30, but with the leaves still on the trees blocking the light, I was aware that the shooting light would go out quickly afterward inside the woods. This would make my window for a sighting smaller than I liked, but I was no less excited because of the limitation.

It was still warm in Tennessee, so I took advantage of my 3:15 arrival at the farm and moved deliberately slowly toward my stand. I did so in order to minimize the odor-carrying sweat that would form on my skin. I knew the dryer my skin and clothes were, the more chance I had of defeating the incredible ability of the nose I was hoping to outsmart. Finally at about 3:40 I was yanking on the rope that I use for pulling my compound bow up to the platform where I would sit. My vantage point was about 18 feet off the ground.

It's hard to describe how sure I felt that I would be coming to full draw before the end of that late September day. While I waited for the moment to come, I checked my release to make sure it was working fine and looked the bow over closely to see if anything looked unusual. I also rechecked my arrow to make sure that the odd color plastic vane had "#1" written on it with black Scripto ink. It was my prize arrow that had earned the top spot among those in my quiver in regard to beauty of flight. It had already proven itself trustworthy at the

3-D deer target in my backyard. My confidence was way up. All I had to do now was wait and watch.

At last it was getting near show time. I could feel it in my anxious bones. As the evening light began to grow slightly dim, I went ahead and attached the release to the string. I wanted to be as ready as possible just in case the thicket would give birth to the beast. The slight wind was coming through the timber in my face and would not be a factor if the deer came in front of me from my left as I hoped it would.

I slowly turned my head from side to side checking both directions as well as straight ahead. My stand was about 20 yards inside the woods, and a well-used trail passed by me at about 10 yards out. I could imagine the deer strolling along the path, nose to the ground, finding the thin-shelled candy that the white oak trees had thrown down.

I had to face the possibility that if the buck felt safe enough he might skirt the field just outside the edge of the woods. But I was prepared if he made that move. Weeks before I had cleared a good size shooting lane from the ladder stand in the acorns all the way to the field edge.

As I checked the opening and mentally rehearsed what would be a 30-yard shot, movement suddenly caught my eye. I saw him! It was the mister that had haunted me all day long. The stranger was still on the farm. I was so right…he was so there, except for one small detail.

Through the openness of the shooting lane I could see all the way across the field to where the stand was located that I had been in that morning. I kid you not—that old buck was walking nearly under it. It looked as though he was out in the soybeans far enough not to be spooked by my scent trail I had left as I walked in and out of the area. He was casually stepping toward another patch of woods at the other end of the farm. I couldn't believe it. So close, yet so far. I whispered, "If I were only over there…"

Darkness came and the only trophy I carried home was the fact that I had at least seen the coveted prize again. Needless to say I was somewhat distracted during the evening. I mentioned the encounter to Annie briefly. I think she knew that my pensiveness meant that in my mind I was still in the woods in the pursuit, and that I was making my plans to return to the farm before daylight came again. Thankful for a schedule that would allow it, along with a wife who understands my…well…my obsession, as well as a nest that had been empty of kids for a couple of years, I seized the freedom and schemed a predawn return to the farm. The debate that went on in my head that night about where to set up the next morning was fierce.

"I should go back to the stand in the acorn trees tomorrow morning."

"No, you should go back and set up at the other end in the stand where you were when you first saw him this morning. Don't forget, he went by there this evening. He might come back by there tomorrow morning."

"No, don't forget the acorns. There's way too many nuts falling for him to ignore. I should stay in the oak grove."

"But you saw him on the other end…"

I nearly drove myself wacko with the brain bickering over how to hunt the buck the next day. But I finally made a decision. As wise as it might have been to get back in the stand in the acorns that I sat in that evening, I succumbed to trying to "chase" the buck and chose the field-edge stand where I had seen him last. As it turned out, it didn't matter.

I did see the buck again the next morning but he was not close to either of the two stands that have been mentioned. He stepped out of a small island-like thicket that borders the field about halfway between the ladder stand on one end of the field and the acorn tree-patch stand on the other end. He fed for about ten minutes in the soybeans and wandered back into it, probably to bed down. The sighting was brief, but it packed a long-term wallop on my psyche. My determination to outwit the deer jumped into high gear. I was committed. On the drive home I rehearsed how I would grovel about wanting to go back yet again to hunt that afternoon. The groveling worked!

Guess where I was that evening. Yep. You're absolutely correct. I was at the edge of the middle thicket where I had seen him that morning. I knew it was a good hiding place. In fact, I knew it so well that I had already placed a stand there in July, long before season had opened. So it was no trouble to slip into it for an ambush. Once again I slowly made my way to the edge of the island thicket to minimize the moisture that formed on my skin. Knowing the thicket was a rather small hiding place and that any odd sounds could be heard very well, I made sure my ascent up the climbing stick and onto the lock-on stand was as quiet as possible. One metal-on-metal ding and I knew my presence would be known. The Velcro connections on my string release straps were a special challenge to keep silent. It took me every bit of two minutes to open it up in order to attach it to my hand. I did everything right. However, once again, it was to no avail because that evening I didn't see him at all. My diligence to details was not rewarded. Assuming he exited the opposite side of the thicket, I reluctantly made my dismount when the last light of twilight faded.

"Instandity"

I think by now you're getting the picture of the multistand madness I created for myself that season. I actually had seven permanently mounted stands on the farm to choose from. With so many choices, I eventually used at least five of the locations during my frenzied but unsuccessful chasing of the big buck. I can't recall how many times I was set up here and he showed up over there, only to set up there and see him here, then I'd go there and see him yet over yonder.

To further prove how insanely fixated on the chase I had become, on more than one occasion I did something totally incoherent. I would get in a stand and sit there a few minutes, look across the field at another place that I thought might hold more promise, and then would actually climb out and move to it. My antics had truly turned ridiculous.

I chased that old buck enough that I think I totally ran him off to another county. He may have still been on the farm, but if he was I had motivated him to be so nocturnal that the hope of seeing him again during legal shooting light grew more and more bleak. In fact, the season closed without another single sighting—not even during gun season.

When something that happens while I'm hunting is as emotionally significant to me as my failed, frenzied chase, I will usually reflect on it enough to at least find a trophy of truth in it. And most often the insight is more valuable than the mount that could have resulted (and far less expensive in terms of a taxidermy bill!). But there's a reason I look for the lesson. It is because there have been things I've learned about my character or personality that I've discovered while hunting that have benefited me greatly when I carried the insight out of the woods and into the rest of my life.

For example, in the book *A Look at Life from a Deer Stand,*

I wrote about the self-inflicted danger a rut-driven buck can put himself in when he abandons his normally cautious nature to pursue a receptive doe. In the same way if a man allows an unrestrained reaction to his hormonal drive, he is asking to be shot at with the bullet of an immoral temptation. A revealing snapshot like this taken in the hunter's woods is a precious and valuable picture that, when studied, can yield a stronger moral character in a man.

The importance of what I learned from stepping back and seriously looking at how I tried to outsmart the elusive buck by wildly hopping around from stand to stand taught me something monumental. Basically, I made the mistake of letting the hunt become about me and not about meat.

One of my cardinal rules as a hunter is simple but not always an easy one to follow: The primary reason for pursuing the whitetail is to feed physical hunger, not to feed an emotional appetite for the undeniable thrill of outwitting a mature and intelligent animal like the one that taunted me with its ghostly appearances. While I firmly believe this is a worthy and noble approach to the quest, I am very much aware that the competition that can erupt between a hunter and an old woods-savvy buck can be one of the most exciting reasons to head to the woods. I would not be honest to deny this dynamic of deer hunting. However, there is a dangerous ingredient, if added to the mix, that can poison the pie. That deadly ingredient is called bragging rights.

Among those who pursue the whitetail, it is an unspoken reality that a large rack can mean serious attention for a hunter, and the praises that accompany the kill can be quite intoxicating. Believing that dragging home a deer with a massive set of antlers would testify to my hunting prowess, I began to entertain thoughts of what glorious things might be said about me if I could just outsmart the old boy. Consequently, the hunger for the burger, back strap, and mild, smoked Italian venison sausage ceased to be my primary enticement for the chase. Instead I became starved to hear friends, family, and other hunters say, "What a man! With only a bow and arrow and his unmatched skills he conquered the beast of beasts of Robertson County, Tennessee!" I even had secret dreams of the day I would be approached by the hunting industry types to beg me to make a mold of the rack I hadn't yet taken. After all, everyone in the deer hunting community knows that "big bucks can equal big bucks!"

Ultimately, and this is hard to admit, my real problem was *pride*. What *I* wanted became more important than following the basics of a smart pursuit. I focused so much on me that I lost the handle on something the apostle Paul mentions in Romans 12:3: "I say to everyone among you not to think more highly of himself than he ought to think; but to think so as to have sound judgment."

Inebriated by the unrealistic fantasies of fame, I allowed myself to abandon the sound judgment of deer hunting basics. Consequently, I managed to hunt completely different than I normally would. If I had been sensible, I would have gone to the area of the farm where the mature deer seemed to favor far less often in order to not contaminate the area with my scent and too frequent presence. Also I would have factored in my knowledge of the layout of the land and determined which thickets would be preferred by such a shrewd deer. Doing so might have led to using only one or maybe two of the stands, according to the prevailing wind on the day of each hunt. With smart hunting, sooner or later the heavy "stranger" would probably have walked under me. Instead, my longing for applause drove me to forsake logical thinking.

Quoting from the writings of Professor William K. Kirkpatrick, "Extreme forms of mental illness are always extreme cases of self-absorption."[5] While I wouldn't go so far as to classify my season-long, multimovement hunting style as a product of mental illness, jumping from one location to another was at least a mild form of "temporary *instandity!*" Thankfully, however, my "hunt-gone-mad" served me well because I can report that since that memorable, regrettable season of craziness, I have managed to calm down and return to sound judgment. Bolstering my image is not on my list of reasons I want to hunt these days. It was a good thing that I did get a grip on reality after that season of silliness, because two years later, a really big one showed up again at the same farm. This time the outcome was quite different. By Tennessee standards he is a bona fide 14 pointer and now in my possession. No brag, just fact.

6

Secret Trophy

The morning was cool and the white of the brilliant stars began to fade as the advancing dawn turned the sky from black to gray-blue. The level of anticipation for what might happen was rising with the sun in Gerald's mind. Within a few minutes the very tops of the trees were outlined with the golden hue of the first rays of sunlight. It was the kind of morning a deer hunter lives to see and feel. Gerald wondered if it could possibly be any better. Then he saw movement in the distance.

It seemed to take forever for the innocent to be proven guilty. Sure enough, it was a walking deer that had caught his keen eye. Moving cautiously just inside the woods, a whitetail skirted the edge of the field and then stepped slightly into it. As it stood motionless with only its head showing, Gerald slowly lifted his binoculars to his eyes to take a closer look. His heart raced with excitement at what he saw. It was a sizable buck.

The main beams of the deer's antlers extended out well beyond its ears. The height of the brow tines appeared to be at least six inches or better. The G2's stood even taller and the set was nearly perfect in symmetry.

Gerald knew well that studying the rack so closely was risky. Only one time before had such a large whitetail presented an opportunity for the taking, but Gerald fell victim to the disease of "buck fever" and it had cost him the trophy of a lifetime. That mistake had nagged at him for far too long, and the lesson he learned about the importance of focusing on the kill zone instead of the brag zone kicked in. He gingerly pulled the binoculars away from his eyes.

He could feel his hands starting to shake as he gripped his rifle. Without taking his eyes off the deer he nervously felt for the safety lever and gently laid his gloved thumb on it. As if he believed he could telepathically speak to the heavy deer, he whispered through his lips that had quickly turned dry, "Come on, Big Guy, step on out so I can see all of you."

At that same moment, as though the deer had received the message, it took about eight steps into the meadow and stood only slightly quartered toward Gerald. The morning sun lit up the enormous set of antlers like a spotlight, tempting the hunter to lose his concentration. Determined to not falter in the basics, Gerald set his gaze on the deer's body and refused to look away. But the angle of the deer's stance made the target much too small.

"Turn, Big Boy, turn." Gerald quietly begged the buck to step either right or left and present him with a broadside shot. At this point, the view he had of the deer included the crosshairs of his scope. With his elbows resting on the railing of his climbing treestand providing a steady hold, he peered through the lenses and studied the distance from the end of his barrel to the buck: *175, maybe 190 max. That's close enough!*

Gerald pushed the safety lever forward and revealed the small circle of red that warns of impending doom for anything that stands in the scope's field of view. His heart pounded as he felt for the trigger. "Wait! Wait! He's gotta be completely broadside. Do the right thing." The teacher of experience was coaching as Gerald waited and hoped for the deer to turn.

His heart raced even faster when he noticed that the deer's demeanor suddenly turned somewhat nervous as he took about five more slow steps and turned to the right. Fearing that the huge buck was about to return to the shadows of the timber, he felt convinced it was time to take the shot. With his scope set at its highest level of magnification, he placed the fine lines of the crosshairs at the top edge of the deer's lung area to compensate for the distance.

"It's time. This is it! Hold steady. Squeeze. Let the kick be a surprise."

The report of Gerald's large caliber rifle resounded throughout the long valley, but he didn't hear it. Nor did he feel the sharp impact of the gun on his shoulder when it recoiled in response to the explosion. He felt strangely numb as he watched the buck crumple to the ground right where it had been standing. He quickly bolted another cartridge and kept the safety on the off position. With his index finger poised softly on the trigger and the crosshairs firmly on what little bit he could see of the deer, he waited an entire minute making sure that the monstrous buck had yielded its life to a well-placed shot.

Convinced that he had effectively connected with his target, Gerald slid the safety back to the on position and lowered his rifle, resting it on the railing of his stand. He sat motionless as the gentle warmth of the rising sun touched his back. He was stunned. He wanted to celebrate, but he couldn't. He wanted to dismount the tree and run to the massive animal he had just taken, but he knew he shouldn't. And there was a very good reason that he hesitated to do either of these things. Between him and the expired buck was a fence.

Gerald replayed the recent moments that he had just lived and shook his head in disbelief. "Why did you do that? Why didn't you wait?" His whisper sounded exasperated. "Surely that ol' boy would have jumped that barbed wire. Just a few more yards and you wouldn't be feeling this way right now. You could have waited!"

The jubilation he should have been feeling was replaced with a troublesome churning in his gut. The fence that his bullet had sailed over divided two farmers' properties, and the land on the other side was strictly off limits to Gerald. One of the conditions that he had agreed to with the man who owned the farm he was permitted to hunt was to never trespass on the neighboring land with neither body nor bullet.

He tried every argument he could think of to justify his decision to shoot. None of them worked to squelch the ugly sound of self-loathing he was hearing in his head. Realizing that he had no defense for what he had done, he resorted to an idea that made a lot of sense at first. "You don't have to tell that you shot it on the other side of that fence. Just put the deer on this side when you tell your story. What's the harm?" he said out loud.

Gerald thought about the scheme of concocting a revamped story but quickly decided it would not be something he would want to tell over and over. He searched fast and hard for another option. It took a minute or two for the idea to come to him, but at last he decided what he would do.

"I don't have to tell a soul about this buck. Not one friend—not even my wife. This can be my private trophy. No one has to know! I won't even check this deer in. My wife will be at work all day. I'll quickly load the buck in the truck and butcher it in the barn…" Gerald stopped in mid-thought then realized, "No, I can't do that, how will I explain the fresh meat in the freezer?"

Gerald was appalled by his next thought, but he accepted it as the best option. "I'll saw the rack off and dump the carcass. That's what I'll do. That's what I have to do!"

Gerald roused himself out of the regret that was growing larger by the minute and began to closely examine the surrounding area, looking for other spots of blaze orange. He made a complete 360 degree, radar-like turn and saw no evidence of another hunter nearby. Feeling sure he was alone, he began the dismount procedure, all the while begging the air that no one would show up during his retrieval of his secret trophy. He didn't feel like he could ask God for that favor.

Once on the ground, and with his gun and detached climber leaning against the tree, he quickly headed toward the downed buck. As he hurried he continued to make full circle inspections of the area wanting to be sure he was not being watched. When he crossed the barbed wire fence he was close enough to the deer to see that its antlers stood well above the tall grass in which it laid.

"Unbelievable!" he whispered and then did the radar turn again as he squatted down to hold the huge rack. A half smile came to his face as he gripped the base of the heavy antlers. He could barely get his hands around them. Then he shook himself out of the momentary admiration, grabbed the left side of the main beams and began to hurriedly drag the heavy carcass toward the treestand where his belongings waited.

"No time to marvel. I gotta get this deer to the truck and do it quick." The voice seemed to be someone else's, but he responded with an urgency that made him feel strangely nervous.

Exhausted and sweating profusely Gerald dropped the rack into the leaves under the tree that he had hunted from that morning. "I can get the truck real close. This is gonna work," he whispered as he turned and headed to his pickup. The brisk pace he kept was accompanied by more careful searches of the area to be further sure that his plans would not be monitored by an onlooker.

The metal ramp system he had created to self-hoist a deer into his truck bed worked beautifully. With the hacksaw cleaned and put away in his tool box, the deer safely hidden under a tarp, and the topper lid closed and locked, Gerald drove toward his home. On the way he made one very quick stop on a remote section of the gravel road that led him to the main highway. He felt sick at his stomach as the heavy body of the deer slid down into the deep ditch.

When he pulled away from the dump sight he looked in his rearview mirror to make sure there were no other vehicles in sight. Feeling confident that he had flown under the radar with his plan, he headed home.

As he drove along, he thought of all the buddies who would love to have seen the brute that he had taken. As the names of his friends went through his mind, he wondered what they would have said about his find…but they would never get the chance. Then he thought of his wife, Mary, and his son, Sam, and his spirit sank as low as he could ever remember.

Gerald spoke out loud to himself over the hum of the truck engine, "How am I ever going to hide this morning from Mary? She knows me well enough to detect my attempts to keep something from her. This is not going to be easy. I'll have to be careful. I can keep this to myself. That's what I gotta do…but what about Sam? He'll be crushed if he ever finds out about this. He can never, ever see the rack." The thought pushed him even further into the pit of sadness.

The evening came and dinner was placed on the table. Gerald laughed with Mary as she drank her after-dinner cup of coffee and told him about something funny that had happened with one of the students at the school that day. He bantered with Sam about a news story they watched. During a lull in the conversation Gerald petted the family dog that sat on his lap and carefully examined the faces of his family. He had to know if they showed any signs at all of suspicion. They didn't, and he felt relief. But the next words he heard were painful to hear.

"See anything this morning, dad?" Gerald dreaded the question that he was afraid Sam would ask.

"I saw absolutely one of the prettiest sunrises I have seen in my entire life, " Gerald responded, clawing at his mind for a diversion. He put his hand up in the "wait a second" position and said, "Excuse me, Sam."

Then he looked toward the kitchen and asked, "Mary! Are we still going to your mother's this weekend?"

Sam assumed that his dad's morning was shot-less as he heard his mother say, "Yep. She's expecting us."

Sam attempted to console his dad with, "Bet you're looking forward to that trip, hey Pop?"

Gerald felt relief again. He had successfully sidetracked

the conversation. Nothing else was said about the hunt, and the evening went on. Finally he went to bed and put his head on his pillow. In the darkness he replayed the unforgettable morning he had experienced, as well as the many emotions that accompanied it. He was tired both in body and spirit. The last thoughts he had before drifting off to sleep were a mental picture of a large deer carcass sliding into the deep ravine at the side of the remote gravel road on the other side of the county and the tortured sight of a 12-point rack buried deep behind a pile of worthless junk that hadn't been moved in the barn for nearly 15 years. "I should've just tossed the whole thing over the hill. That's what I should have done." But he hadn't, and sleep didn't come easy.

It is obvious that by trying to secretly hold on to his record-book rack Gerald had created far more trouble for himself than it was worth. But that's what happens when we conceal a treasure that has been wrongly obtained. It usually yields nothing but turmoil. As hard as he tried, Gerald would never totally enjoy his secret trophy. He was not the first to face such a dilemma. His story has a familiar ring to it. It sounds hauntingly like the biblical account of a man named Achan in the Old Testament book of Joshua.

Israel had conquered Jericho and Joshua placed a ban on the spoils of the victory. He allowed only certain items to be collected by the people and told them if any one of them violated the ban, God would deal harshly with the entire nation of Israel. Sadly, a man among their ranks ignored Joshua's command and put the whole nation at risk by his thievery and deception. God divinely revealed to Joshua that Israel had been made weak by the wickedness of one among them. The search for the owner of the sin led to Achan. We'll pick up the story in Joshua, verse 19 of chapter 7:

> Then Joshua said to Achan, "My son, I implore you, give glory to the Lord, the God of Israel, and give praise to Him; and tell me now what you have done. Do not hide it from me."
>
> So Achan answered Joshua and said, "Truly, I have sinned against the Lord, the God of Israel, and this is what I did: when I saw among the spoil a beautiful mantle from Shinar and two hundred shekels of silver and a bar of gold fifty shekels in weight, then I coveted them and took them; and behold, they are concealed in the earth inside my tent with the silver underneath it."
>
> So Joshua sent messengers, and they ran to the tent; and behold, it was concealed in his tent with the silver underneath it. They took them from inside the tent and brought them to Joshua and to all the sons of Israel, and they poured them out before the Lord (Joshua 7:19-23).

Achan paid an awful price for his sin but he didn't pay alone. He and his family were stoned to death. Their harsh punishment was a strong warning to everyone in the nation that they should never allow their greed to cause them to forget God's laws.

Though the story of the infamous "sin of Achan" is ancient, it is a timeless lesson about how coveting can lead to stealing. But in Achan's case, stealing is not where it stopped. *Concealing* was his next step, and his actions bear a striking resemblance to what Gerald did. Both of these men obtained the objects of their desire but knowing that they had gotten them wrongfully, each of them felt compelled to hide their treasures.

For both men, the items that once had so great a value were reduced to nothing but heavy burdens. Being driven by the need to cover their transgressions, one buried his stolen treasure under the dirt inside his tent, the other buried his trophy behind dusty junk in his barn. The dirt and the junk are pictures of the pile of lies that had to be told to hide their sins.

Someone wise once said, "It is far better to want what you don't have than to have what you don't want." I can't help but think that even though Achan slept near his treasures and ate with them under his feet, he would have traded them for peace of mind. Yet he kept them even though they were worthless as long as they were buried. He held on to them even though no one could ooh or ah at the sight of the prizes.

Gerald did the same thing with the antlers that had caught his eye on that gloriously beautiful autumn morning. Essentially he coveted what belonged to another man according to the rules of boundaries. He ignored the inner warning that said, "You should wait! Give the deer a chance to jump the fence. If he does, then he's rightfully yours." Instead, feeling he just had to have the spoils of another's land and fearing that a chance at such a huge deer may never come again, he pulled the trigger of disobedience. His heart was the first to trespass on the other man's property, but then his bullet and eventually his body crossed the fence. So many rules had been broken. The rack got to him, and he had to have it.

Such can be the case for other things men and women have been known to covet, catch, and then conceal. Consider, for example, the married men or women who hide affairs. Though they feel they just have to have that other person, like Achan and Gerald realized, once they enter the arena of unfaithfulness they feel like they have to bury or hide the relationship. They shudder at the thought of anyone finding out. They live in fear of accidentally saying the wrong name or mentioning a place they've been but never with their spouses. The irony of it is that the value of the other person who was once so desirable diminishes as the fear of being found out steadily grows.

The stories of Achan and Gerald and their similar transgressions beg for two questions to be answered: What can be done in advance to avoid the consequences of the sin of coveting and covering up? If there is something already buried under the dirt and junk of lies, what can be done to break free from the burden that hiding them has placed on the heart?

Both men would have done well to know the answer to the first question. So would the rest of us who have concealed objects of unfaithful affection. Perhaps the best way to avoid this grave error is to maintain a deep abiding fear of God, the kind that can keep us from making the wrong choice in the first place! The motivation must be a godly fear that is based on an unwavering belief that He is serious about His people obeying His commandments. If we truly accepted the truth that sin will surely be rewarded with harsh consequences, would we not see in advance of coveting a thing that the pleasure of having it is just not worth the pain? Surely we would!

But Achan dismissed the warning about the consequences that Joshua promised to all the people of Israel—and I wonder why. Perhaps he convinced himself he could get away with the treasures. Maybe he figured he could mark the spot where he had buried them and someday go back to that place after sufficient time had passed. Then, when he returned, he could uncover and enjoy the spoils of the battle. Ultimately I don't know how he managed to ignore a warning as stern as the one given by his leader, but one thing is for sure: Achan allowed his lust for the treasures to take the place of the respect he had for Joshua's authority.

Achan could have very well made his mistake because he forgot, or ignored, one eternal truth: His every move was being observed by the God of Israel, the Authority to whom Joshua submitted, the very God who will in eternity judge every man for what is done within the framework of time. If Achan had held on to this reality, his actions would surely have been different.

It is amazing how differently people behave when they realize the eyes of authority are watching. If you've ever been driving down the highway and suddenly looked in the rear-view mirror and discovered a policeman tailing your car, you know what usually happens—you make a quick and nervous assessment of how well you are driving. You immediately look at your speedometer, you grip the wheel a little tighter, and you carefully avoid any side to side movements. You make sure your seat belt is fastened, you wonder if the date on your license plate is current, and you pray that your brake lights and turn signals work if you have to use them.

How much more should care be given to our actions if we believe that the eyes of God are observing our every move and that He sees each transgression? If we're ever tempted to doubt that God has us in His view, we can run to at least three passages of Scripture that confirm He is always right behind us on the highway of life.

In Psalms there is a recorded prayer of Moses: "You have placed our iniquities before You, our secret sins in the light of Your presence" (90:8). Jeremiah 16:17 warns, "For My eyes are on all their ways; they are not hidden from My face, nor is their iniquity concealed from My eyes." Proverbs 5:21 instructs, "For the ways of a man are before the eyes of the LORD, and He watches all his paths."

It might be wise to post these verses on our fridges, on the dashes of our vehicles, and for those of us who hunt big game as guests on borrowed land, we could write the passages on the stocks of our guns or the risers of our bows and think about them carefully. And we would all be wise to always remember that the God of the ages, the one and only Creator of all that surrounds us here and beyond, the One who is omnipotent and all-knowing, who reigns over the universe, this awesome God sees even the most carefully hidden sins in our lives. While it may be frightening to realize this truth, it can also be encouraging to realize that God's watchful eyes can be the very thing that can strengthen us when we're faced with temptation. If we truly and fearfully believe that He's watching our every move, we would surely be motivated to resist the deadly urge to "send the bullet of our desire to the other side of the fence."

Certainly the sobering knowledge that God sees us clearly and at all times can stir us to righteous decisions. But what happens if the trigger of willful disobedience has already been pulled? What could Achan have done, or Gerald do, to know peace and to calm the raging storm of turmoil caused by foolishly giving in to coveting, then getting, and then burying? The answer is to uncover the secret trophy. Bring it out of hiding. Come clean. When a transgressor owns the sin, it won't own the sinner. Humble, voluntary repentance would have been the high road for Achan to take, but sadly he didn't. He was forced to confession by Joshua's revelation from God. It's too late for Achan. For Gerald, however, it is still an option, one that could yield a trophy of far greater value than a rack of skull and bone. He would find the prizes of forgiveness and peace.

What deep relief Gerald would know if he would go into his barn, get the antlers, load them into his truck, and take a drive to the homes of the farmers whose good graces were so abused. Then, with camo hat in hand, he could humbly offer a sincere apology with something like "I have wronged you. I have broken the rules I was supposed to hunt by. I beg you to forgive me. And it would be just fine if I never set foot on this part of the county again. I am here to ask for your mercy and forgiveness." I have no doubt that if Gerald made such an admission to the landowner, and to God as well, he could go home free from the burden of his secret trophy. And when it came time to sleep again he would find that…there is no softer pillow than a conscience that is clear.

> I acknowledged my sin to You, and my iniquity I did not hide. I said, "I will confess my transgressions to the LORD"; and You forgave the guilt of my sin.
>
> PSALM 32:5

7

Don't Unpack Your Bags

Watching the long line of whitetails file into the field was sort of like watching the members of a congregation enter a church. One by one, right after daylight, they walked into their clover-laden sanctuary. It was another October sunrise service for the members of the First Herd of Giles County. Little did they know that an outsider was hidden among the decoration of foliage that formed the perimeter of their four-acre chapel. He was watching every move they were making as they bowed their heads to partake of the offering of nutrition on the floor of the field.

Among the members were at least a dozen mature females and several youngsters. They were grazing together near the center of the sanctuary. A few yards away were three adolescent, short-antlered males that fed intentionally close to the main group. Not too far from them was another gent who looked a little older. Though his beams had more mass and he was obviously the most advanced in age, he seemed a bit too young to be considered a patriarch. Still, there was a certain vigor in his demeanor that indicated he was at least in some leadership capacity. In keeping with the church metaphor, he could be referred to as the pastor.

While the members milled around and enjoyed their fellowship meal of clover and other tender grasses at their feet, the largest of the males, the pastor, started acting a little nervous. He stood motionless and peered toward the door through which he and the congregation had entered their haven. Because that kind of tentative behavior in a male whitetail usually indicates that he has detected the presence of an approaching intimidator, there was no guessing at what troubled him. Sure enough, arriving typically and intentionally late to the morning meeting was the self-appointed leader of the group.

With his head high and sporting a massive throne of antlers, his neck stiff and swelled, he walked into the sanctuary a few yards and stopped. He looked toward the assembly of females first, then his eyes went to the few young men that were standing around looking at him and acting noticeably edgy. Just behind them was the pastor. He too had his gaze fixed worriedly on the latecomer.

After standing there for about 30 or 40 motionless seconds, the sizeable, seasoned whitetail looked once more at the ladies then began majestically strolling toward the men. There was a threatening air in the way he walked. After he took only a few steps toward them, all the young guys scattered to other parts of the chapel, leaving only the pastor to deal with the heavy "elder."

Suddenly the old man lowered his head, darted toward the young buck, and a confrontation of major proportions erupted. The battering noise of their intermingling head gear filled the cathedral. While it was music to the hunter's ears, the pastor was probably not feeling so fond of the aggressive hits he was taking to both his body and his ego.

For what seemed three or four minutes the two males

fought, going in circles as they did, throwing dirt and grass with their hooves as they dug in and lunged toward each other, only to separate and do it again. It was obvious that the blows were not equal in their effectiveness. The elder's body was heavier, and he seemed much more skilled at throwing his weight around. The tattered younger male was beginning to weaken in the fray.

The hunter sat in his secret perch, stunned but quietly engrossed in the battle he was watching. However, what happened next made him cringe with horror and sympathy. With a force that is unimaginable the old antlered member of the congregation buried two of his lengthy tines into the young fellow's neck and jaw area. There was an audible moan as the seriously wounded fighter struggled to detach himself from his aggressor.

Bleeding and battered the poor young pastor stumbled, then gathered what wits he had remaining and limped off toward the back door of the church. All alone he disappeared into the morning mist, probably to lay down and die.

The brute elder panted slightly as he stood and watched his victim make an exit from his presence. Feeling quite sure that there would be no other challengers, especially among the very young boys who had just witnessed the power he wielded, the elder strolled triumphantly toward the ladies. It was their turn to be nervous.

Most deer hunters, if they spend enough time in the stand, will eventually observe this kind of battle. In the world of the whitetail (and many other antlered beasts), what took place between the "pastor" and "the elder" is totally normal behavior. A big buck's nature is to gain dominance over the younger, smaller bucks in a herd. The reward for his aggressive antics is that he gets to be first in line to pass on his strong genes. But as common a sight as these antler wars can be, there is still a certain sorrow a hunter feels for the younger guy that gets his whitetail whooped by the brute of the bunch, especially if the beating is physically fatal or at least results in a seriously injured sense of dignity.

Whenever I think of the gravely wounded buck that was referred to as "the pastor," I am prone to think of another pastor of the human kind whose story has some similarities. He too has a firsthand understanding of the hurt that can be rendered by an older buck who seeks to gain dominance in a congregation. And though the turf wars are a fully natural aspect of deer behavior, what happened to our pastor friend is not supposed to take place among people who lead in the church of the living God. In support of this young preacher, I wrote an adaptation of his story into a song. The lyric was born during a dinner that Annie and I had with him and his wife.

James and Sherry (not their real names) were nearly in tears as they held each other's hands and told us their dilemma. They had moved from a rather large city to a small town in a neighboring state only because they both were absolutely sure God had led them to do so. The pastorate held great promise for growth, and the town was a ripe field waiting to be harvested for the Lord. So with their four small children in tow, they packed up and made the move.

They arrived at their new church and enjoyed being immediately embraced by their new friends and spiritual family. As a man who was relatively young in his calling, the husband was grateful and excited to have the honor of leading such a well-established congregation. He stepped confidently into the pulpit and all was going really great…until one day just three months into his new pastorate something dreadful happened. The dark spirit of an "elder" showed up.

The trouble started when the young preacher addressed a subject in his sermon that, until he arrived at the church, had been taboo. Though the truth in his Sunday morning message was delivered in a carefully gentle way, it was without question a definite challenge to the congregation to think and pray about it. However, when Monday morning came, word had swept through the church office that "the elder" was on his way to meet with the pastor, and he wasn't happy. The problem for the preacher was that the man who would be confronting him was entrenched in the church as an influential figure. In fact, he was the very one who had managed to keep the previous pastors in check about the socially controversial issue that the new preacher had covered the day before. Add to that, his influence in the small community enhanced the level of intimidation he was known to use inside the walls of the church.

The young pastor stood at his office window watching the parking lot, waiting like a nervous young buck for the dominant buck to enter the field. He knew a battle for position was about to ensue.

The meeting didn't last long, and the pastor managed to hold his ground in regard to his message about the biblical stance on the issue. He apologized that his sermon had offended the elder and strongly suggested they bring their dispute before the entire leadership as soon as possible. The elder was not agreeable and left the meeting abruptly.

Though their encounter spanned just a few minutes, the effects lingered on into the weeks ahead. Rumors about the pastor using church funds for questionable personal purposes floated around, along with other chatter about suspicious behavior that he was allegedly concealing. There wasn't a shred of truth about the gossip, but the damage was being done. Though the pastor could not be certain, he was justified in his assumptions about the source of the rumors that were being spread. Wisely, however, he made no formal accusations.

As Annie and I shared a meal with the preacher and his wife, our hearts were broken as the couple confided in us about the severity of the emotional wounds they were feeling due to the false tales that were being told. Without revealing names or intricate details about the staff wars that were being fought between Sundays, it was obvious from their tortured expressions that they were worried about how much longer they could endure the beating they were taking. Their words also revealed that they had serious doubts about their longevity in the town, even though their presence had been so brief.

We were impressed with the amount of discretion each of them showed in regard to not naming names. It was obvious that the reason they came to us was not to return evil for evil but to get some neutral advice from someone who was not only older but who was also detached from the church and could offer an objective view.

As they wiped their eyes, Annie and I realized they were desperately hungry to hear some encouragement. That's when my very astute wife cut to the very core of the matter. She looked at the emotionally tired couple and began talking, addressing most of her comments to the pastor.

"I don't know who the person is who has shown such opposition and who may very well have started the rumors, but it seems to me that what you're dealing with here is a 'Diotrephes.' You probably already know about his legacy in 3 John. Let me simply remind you that he was the one who, according to verse 9, loved 'to be first' among the brethren, and refused to accept what John had to say."

Annie went to our office, got her New American Standard Bible, came back to the dining room and laid it on the table. "I want to get it right so I'll read it. This is what John wrote about Diotrophes. I think you'll agree that the spirit of this text sounds familiar. John said, 'For this reason, if I come, I will call attention to his deeds which he does, unjustly accusing us with wicked words; and not satisfied with this, he himself does not receive the brethren, either, and he forbids those who desire to do so and puts them out of the church.'"

Our guests' faces made it quite clear that the scenario in the Scriptures did indeed sound all too familiar. They both looked at each other and nodded their heads in unison, agreeing that "the elder" seemed to fit the mold of Diotrophes. The once energetic but now subdued preacher spoke up.

"What would you suggest we do, Annie? We really love the area, our kids love it, and we really did feel called to the place we are. What should we do?"

I know to be quiet when my Bible-scholarly wife is given the opportunity to respond to a question so loaded with a need to be answered. She grinned and responded as she often does when the Scriptures are opened. She said, "Read on!"

Addressing the pastor at our table specifically, Annie said, "Verse 11 will guide you about what to do. It says, 'Beloved, do not imitate what is evil, but what is good. The one who does good is of God; the one who does evil has not seen God.'"

Annie started turning backward in the pages of her Bible as she said, "Pastor, your response to this situation is to do good. It may be tempting to lash back with words, but that would be imitating what is evil. You must keep in mind that the one who is causing you so much trouble and dividing the leadership is likely a person who has not seen God. In other words, the bottom line is that he may not be a true believer. I can say that because the fruit of the actions is obviously evil. The fruit is certainly not good. And just to offer you this insight, you can count on the very good likelihood that the evil that drives him has moral implications because in the original language of the passage, the usage of the phrase 'does evil,' ultimately has to do with morality issues. Your sermon that triggered your adversary's ire may have addressed the exact moral issue that plagues him or at least affects someone he is very close to, someone he may prefer to defend. Who knows? But for whatever reason, you're dealing here with a doer of evil, not a doer of good."

Making sure that her Bible was turned to Matthew 13, Annie looked again at the couple and continued. "Folks, the bad news is, as much as you may want to do it, you can't toss this guy out of the church. He's a tare, and, according to the passage here in Matthew 13:24-30, you are required to let the tares grow with the wheat and to trust God with the separating and burning of the tares. The hazard of inheriting a field of wheat is that with it you get the tares that were intentionally planted there by the devil himself long before you arrived. And if you pull up the tares you will probably uproot some of the innocent, precious stalks of wheat in the church. That's a disaster you want to avoid. Only God can do the kind of separating that does not result in harm being done to His precious ones."

The preacher pursed his lips and sighed deeply as he responded. "I can't tell you how many nights I've lain awake just staring into the darkness, rehearsing what I'd like to say to this fellow as well as those he has convinced to side with him.

And I'll admit the words aren't pretty nor is the spirit I'd like to deliver them with. I know you're right, Annie, to remind me that I can't fight evil with evil. It's not the way of our Savior. But quite honestly, I don't think I have any more cheeks to turn."

Annie closed her Bible, leaned forward, and in a caring, gentle, somewhat motherly tone she said, "It is obvious to me that you are a man who wants to do good and not evil. The fact that you have shown us your wounded heart without uncovering the name of the one who hurt you is proof to me that you are a man of integrity. You are to be commended for following the biblical order to overcome evil with good. It's an absolute shame that the worst storms some preachers face too often start right in the pews of the church. It should not be so. There are souls sinking deeper into the muddy mire of hopelessness while these kinds of conflicts distract the soul winners. It simply is wrong."

The young shepherd and his wife nodded their heads in agreement. What came next from Annie's heart was the wisdom that sparked the idea to write a ballad to highlight the plight of the preacher who sat at our table, as well as the many others who have unfortunate stories just like his.

Annie continued, "You haven't been at the church too long and the conflict you have encountered is not of God. Just keep in mind that the troublemaker may attempt to control the pulpit, but he will not rule heaven. Even if it doesn't happen until the end of the age, God will see to it that the tare will someday be separated from the wheat and be burned up. May He have mercy on the man's soul and save him from such a fate. But until then, I urge you, pastor, to not stop doing good. Good will win. And whatever you do, don't back down from sharing the truth of God's Word in your sermons. You know as well as I do that it is the only thing that will free the people. But I have to warn you, until this conflict is resolved, if you plan to keep preaching the truth, don't unpack your bags!"

The young pastor smiled as if Annie's words had lit the fuse of his determination to dig in and do battle. I mentally began writing. The following ballad was eventually written to help him keep the fuse burning.

Don't Unpack Your Bags
The new preacher walked up on the porch
Knocked on that old screen door
Waited until the light came on
Said, "Good evening,' Ma'am, I'm Pastor John
I just came by to say hello,
Take a minute and let you know
I just moved here to your fine town
And I start next Sunday morning."

She stepped out in the evening air
Sat down in an old oak chair
Said, "Young man, you seem so nice
But could I give you my advice
Preachers have come to that church for years
They've come with smiles, they leave with tears
One by one like a sad parade
And I offer you this warnin'

"Touch a feather to their ear
Tell them what they wanna hear
Give 'em milk, don't give 'em meat
Make it short and make it sweet
If you wanna stay around
That's what you'll have to do
But don't unpack your bags, young man,
If you plan to preach the truth."

Don't Unpack Your Bags

She said, "I don't go to that church no more
There's something dark behind those doors
First time they rang that steeple bell
They must have heard it down in hell
'Cause they sent their minions to that place
And they hide behind the human faces
Of those who would trade your soul and mine
For just a taste of power.
So you better…

"Touch a feather to their ear
Tell them what they wanna hear
Give 'em milk, don't give 'em meat
Make it short and make it sweet
If you wanna stay around
That's what you'll have to do
But don't unpack your bags, young man
If you plan to preach the truth."

She said, "Now you may wonder how I know
It's 'cause a preacher came here years ago
I loved the way he shined the light
On what was wrong and what was right
We fell in love and we planned to walk that aisle
But they tore him down and stole his smile
He carried that pain to an early grave
It's been hard to be forgiving.
So you better…

"Touch a feather to their ear
Tell them what they wanna hear
Give 'em milk, don't give 'em meat
Make it short and make it sweet
If you like this little town
That's what you'll have to do
But don't unpack your bags, young man
If you plan to preach the truth."[1]

8

Patterned

Not more than two miles from my residence is a neighbor's 40-acre piece of beautiful Tennessee property that I am privileged to hunt. Though not vast in size, it has all the ingredients a deer and turkey hunter could hope for to cook up an adrenaline pie. There's plenty of thickets where deer can bed, some big oaks that can yield an impressive annual rain of mast in the form of acorns, a substantial stand of cedar trees ideal for roosting birds, and a creek bed that courses through the entire farm. It also has a long and lovely 3-acre field with a hardy crop of clover, a plant highly favored by the farm's unusual number of furred and feathered critters.

With its bounty of herd and birds, and its very short distance from the end of my driveway, I candidly admit that the temptation to frequent the farm reaches embarrassing proportions. And during a recent autumn, it did just that due to some unavoidable circumstances.

As the fall season progressed, so did my busy work schedule. My itinerary prohibited me from investing a lot of interstate highway time to travel to hunting grounds that I enjoy in other counties across our state. In addition to that restriction, I was unable to enjoy the occasional daylight to dark vigils in the deer stand that I absolutely love. All this left me feeling rather deprived (excuse me while I wipe the tears!). It was as though I had a severe itch, and I knew my neighbor's property was one place I could go to scratch it.

It would be almost a shame to admit how many mornings and evenings I hunted that farm during the season. The closeness of it allowed me to be there just before daylight, head home around 8:30 (if no "connections" were made), work all day as fast as I could, and be back in the stand around two hours before sunset. I am glad to report that my obsessive response to the opportunity at least bore some redemptive fruit. Specifically, it was something that happened during a series of evening hunts that birthed a revelation that has had a profound impact on how I view my spiritual life.

Before I reveal the discovery, I concede that the overly regular schedule I was enjoying may seem too excessive to some folks. Yet to others (mostly hunters, I'm sure) it might be enviable. You must understand that Annie's and my nest was empty of children, we had no grandkids at that time, and my sweet wife graciously tolerated the going since I was usually home in the morning about the time the coffee was brewing (at least the second pot). So before you cast me off as an insensitive jerk, keep in mind that conditions were just right for me to keep such an unusual hunting regimen. I am aware that it would not be a routine that a majority could enjoy. I was truly blessed.

Another matter that should be addressed that all serious deer hunters are likely questioning at this moment as they read is what about "over hunting" a place. I know very well that frequenting a farm too much can contaminate it and cause the critters to abandon an area if care is not given to let a place rest from the presence of hunters. It was for that reason that I placed three stands in different areas of the property that covered all the points of deer movement.

I had a lock-on/climbing-stick combo placed back in the timber at the edge of a thicket. There I could monitor the deer that came from nearby corn and soybean fields to bed in the mornings or be there when they got up in the evenings to head back to that same food source.

Along the creek bed I had several shooting lanes cleared around a tall, straight, soft-bark tree that I used for my portable climber-type stand. The deer had a deep trail dug into the banks of the stream where they often crossed. There was nothing like being suspended high above the ground to secretly watch a parade of whitetails as they came through.

I truly looked forward to using each of the trio of stands, but the time restraints I faced made it necessary to favor the location at the edge of the field. I also knew I was ignoring my self-imposed policy of avoiding overuse of a stand, but in this case there were a couple of advantages to breaking the rule.

One, the clover in the field was a major attractant, making the possibility of at least seeing deer much higher. Thus, the needle on the anticipation meter was always higher whenever I was in the ladder stand.

Another reason to favor the field edge was convenience. Because the busyness of the day's chores would often push me far into the afternoon, it was simply more advantageous to squeeze the maximum amount of work out of the day and then hurry to the farm. Upon arrival I could jump out of the truck, quickly change into my camo clothes at the tailgate, grab my bow, and walk the short distance to the stand. When the weather was warm, as it usually is in Tennessee during most of our bow-only season, a brief trek to the tree meant there would be very little odor-producing sweat on my skin that could alert the very sensitive olfactory system of the deer. Because of this, I felt reasonably sure I could slip in and out of that spot without permanently jeopardizing the presence of the critters.

But the best of all reasons to use the field edge stand had as much to do with emotional therapy as the thrill of the hunt. In a flash I could go from the hectic madness of dealing with mind-numbing technology to a near total quiet within mere minutes. That was my favorite part of the deal.

As mentioned, it was during my afternoon sits in the ladder stand that I noticed it. Evening after evening, while I scanned the area for whitetail deer, I would catch a glimpse of movement in the grass way down the field. Almost without fail, right around 5:15, the resident wild turkeys would show up. As if they had Timex watches on their wings and knew the time of day, their heads would appear at nearly the same time each evening, bobbing back and forth, moving right to left in the meadow. One by one, until there were sometimes two dozen or more, they would meander out of the timber on the south side of the field, head to the north side, and enter the woods going toward the stand of tall, mature cedars. Then around six, when all the birds were congregated inside the shadowy cover of the woods, I would hear the vigorous flapping of wings accompanied by the distinct fly-up cackle that turkeys voice when they go to bed. (I'm glad humans weren't designed to do that. Then again, maybe some do. I don't know!) It was always a delightful show to watch and hear on those evenings when I could be there to enjoy it.

Then one midday early in the archery deer season, as I labored in the office, I took a break and walked out to the highway to check our mailbox. As I slowly walked back toward our house I shuffled through the stack of letters, bills, and other mail. Suddenly I saw it. I stopped dead in my tracks and stared at the glorious piece of mail I held in my hands. It was from the Tennessee Wildlife Resources Agency. I knew what it was. It had arrived just as I had hoped. It was my fall season, either-sex, computer drawn turkey permits. I was a winner! My heart leaped with 12-gauge joy.

As I tightly clutched the permit between my thumb and twitching trigger finger, my mind raced to the scene at the ladder stand where I sat and waited for deer. I could see the line of turkeys filing across the field of my mind. And I could see myself slowly pulling up the sleeve of my camo shirt to check the timepiece on my arm that read, once again, 5:15, sometimes 5:30.

I could hardly wait to get to the phone and call my friend Lindsey Williams, who had also entered the same drawing. Sure enough, the mailman had delivered the same good news to his box. I knew we were only a few short weeks away from one of the most memorable moments two friends (who enjoy shopping for a Thanksgiving turkey while wearing full camo) could ever share.

By the time the first day of turkey season came, I had enjoyed several more opportunities to observe the ticking of the "turkey time clock" while waiting on whitetails. One doe was in the freezer, by the way, but the commotion created by arrowing and tracking a deer seemed to have done no damage to the regularity of the turkey parade. The only thing that did change was the hour of their appearance. Due to the closing of Daylight Savings Time, their schedule was moved up by 60 minutes.

I called Lindsey to make sure he would be joining me on the first evening of opening day that was posted on our permits. He was fully on go and on the evening before the fall turkey season began he phoned me and asked, "What time should I be at your place tomorrow afternoon?" With a confidence that was founded on much research, I responded, "If you're here at 2:45, we'll have us a bird somewhere between 3:45 and 4:30."

Because archery season had been in full swing for several weeks, Lindsey and I agreed that it felt a little strange to put our bows on the shelf and dust off the shotguns that had been cased since the ending of spring gobbler season. But with an elevated sense of excitement, the kind that can keep a fellow up the night before a hunt and make it hard to concentrate on a "real job" during the day, we climbed into my pickup around 2:50 and drove the short distance to the farm.

On the way, I verbally rehearsed with Lindsey what I was sure would happen that afternoon and how we would best prepare for the harvest. I said, "We'll set up on the north side of the field back in the woods a bit just at the edge of the cedars. Be sure to listen hard at about 3:40. Listen for light clucking and purring. Right after you hear the first call, get set 'cause it won't be long until you'll begin to see the birds as they cross the field and enter the woods."

I was getting all keyed up just saying it, but I continued, "Make sure you have your gun up on your knee at around 3:40 to keep the movement to a minimum. There's going to be dozens of incredibly talented eyes to bust us. Lay your finger on the safety and enjoy the moment!"

Patterned

Lindsey smiled graciously as he listened to me ramble the instructions he already knew how to follow. He was kind enough to let me say it all out loud because he knew I enjoyed saying it. After I finished he responded with a sort of chuckle in his voice, "You're pretty sure about this hunt, aren't you?"

I grinned with confidence. "Oh, yeah! I know their pattern, and I don't think it's likely to change today."

We took our places in the woods around 3:15. Facing in opposite directions about 30 yards apart, we sat quietly waiting in the heavy shadows of the cedars. I checked my watch...3:30. My ears were tuned in to every sound. The chirps of cardinals, the distinct and annoying screech of the blue jay, and the distant sound of the flow of traffic on I-24 reverberated in my head. I was listening hard. Then I heard it.

The first soft cluck was muffled by the foliage still on the trees, but I knew that sound. And I knew well that it came from across the field we were facing. My heart rate shot to hummingbird levels as I slowly pushed the "call" button on the two-way radio clipped to my shirt. "Lindsey, did you hear that?"

"Yep," came his reply. I could tell by his breathy whisper that his respiratory pace had also quickened.

Though I certainly didn't need to say it to him, it just felt good to announce, "This is it, they're here. Sounds like they're coming by you first. Get ready!"

I slowly moved my hand away from the radio and back to my trigger and waited, confident that I would soon hear the report of my friend's shotgun. And, as though the birds' beaks were tied to a string right where Lindsey was sitting and someone was pulling on it, the woods began to fill up with turkeys of various sizes. There was no need for him to move his gun barrel. All he had to do was wait for supper to walk into his sight path.

My entire body jumped at the sound of the blast from Lindsey's 12-gauge. Turkeys flew and ran in all directions, cackling as they dispersed. The only muscle I moved was my index finger as I slowly clicked off the safety and felt for the trigger. I knew there'd be birds running by me.

Boom! Another sudden explosion filled the woods then quickly settled to the sound of flapping of wings and cackles as the flock took flight. I called Lindsey on the radio and said, "Let's sit quiet and let them recongregate and head to the backside of the farm."

Satisfied that we were alone at last with our tasty successes, Lindsey and I stood up, pulled our face masks down and looked through the woods at each other with an unmistakable "high-five" expression. We gathered our gear and our turkeys, headed to the truck and were back at my house before dark had fallen. It was a hunt that we still like talking about.

It would be several days after that memorable afternoon that I would finally discover the important insight that was gleaned from the experience. It sometimes happens sooner, but in this case I'll admit that I was far too caught up in the moment of the pursuit to be cognizant of the spiritual truth that was available in the "on time turkeys."

About a week after Lindsey and I tagged our two birds, I went back to the same farm in pursuit of deer. As I waited again in the field-edge ladder stand, I was thinking about the turkeys that had provided such an unforgettable hunt and wondered if they would show up once again as usual. Amazingly, that evening the same flock of birds, minus two members, appeared in the meadow around 3:30.

While I witnessed their unwavering commitment to their routine, I couldn't help but look ahead with anticipation to the next year's spring gobbler season. As the birds slowly filed across the meadow, I quietly spoke to the feathered congregation that was gathering in the cedars. "Still singin' the same old tune, are ya? You better be singing a new song come March of next year!"

Ding! I heard the "that sounds familiar" bell, and I realized I had just partially quoted a passage from the Old Testament. I couldn't remember the specific chapter or the exact number of the verse but I knew the text was recorded in the Psalms. I checked my Bible concordance to find the exact location when I got home after dark, and it was Psalm 96:1: "Sing to the Lord a new song."

As I sat quietly on the deer stand that evening, I became increasingly excited about the connection that could be made between the repetitive behavior of the birds and the biblical admonition. It was as clear as the bright Tennessee sky that I hunted under, but the more I thought about it, the more I realized how sobering it was.

Very simply, the mistake the turkeys had made was allowing themselves to be patterned. As woods-wise as that particular species of fowl can be, and as difficult as it is to defeat the unbelievably effective ability of their eyes, I had found a weakness in the turkey's lifestyle. Their devotion to their routine was the breech in their wall of defense.

Had they occasionally altered their point of entry into the cedars or chosen to roost in alternate areas of the territory, I wouldn't have been able to set an ambush for them. Perhaps they had grown overly confident in their routine. After all, they had probably followed it all summer and had no reason to think they couldn't do so into the autumn months. For whatever reason, they were at ease with their evening ritual, unaware that the bitter result would be sweet history for the hunters.

People can be very similar to the "clockwork turkeys." We can find a way (doctrine) that can be right, and follow that trail (liturgy/devotions) daily with amazing consistency. The repetition, however, can lead to a feeling of comfort in doing things only in a certain way (traditions), and eventually we begin to put our trust in the trail. The end result is the very thing that can make even the smartest among us quite vulnerable. A pattern develops. And very often it's the pattern that is being observed by the enemy of our souls, Satan, who "prowls around like a roaring lion, seeking someone to devour" (1 Peter 5:8).

With this picture in my mind, I had to ask myself some probing questions about my spiritual life. *What are the good and right things I try to do regularly in my attempt to pursue holiness?* The answers were obvious. Studying the Scripture, praying, fellowshiping with the saints, giving, and witnessing are some list-toppers. *As beneficial and as necessary to the health of the spirit of the believer as these disciplines are, can they ever be used by the enemy against me?* The answer was surprising.

"Yes!" It can happen when a person's rigid adherence to these worthwhile actions are based on the errant belief that rituals equal righteousness. This deadly assumption was a mistake made by the Scribes and Pharisees.

In Jesus' day, the Scribes and the Pharisees were influential interpreters of the Jewish law that had been handed down from the time of Moses. Their interpretation and strict observance of these rules had become more authoritative and binding than the Mosaic Law itself. And they were quick to require others to follow their customs.

For example, in Mark 7:5 the Scribes and Pharisees' confronted Jesus when they saw His disciples violating their tedious premeal rituals such as washing cups, pitchers, copper vessels, and couches. And they particularly noted that the disciples did not wash their hands in that "special way." They asked Jesus, "Why do your disciples not walk according to the tradition of the elders, but eat bread with unwashed hands?"

Quoting Isaiah, Jesus countered the Scribes and Pharisee's religious spirit and said in verse 6, "This people honors Me with their lips, but their heart is far away from me. But in vain do they worship Me, teaching as doctrines the precepts [traditions] of men." And in verse 9 Jesus further rebukes the Scribes and Pharisees with "You are experts at setting aside the commandment of God in order to keep your tradition." Jesus knew they placed far too much emphasis on minor details such as tithing the tiny mint leaves they grew in their gardens while at the same time ignoring the weightier provisions of the law such as "justice and mercy and faithfulness" as mentioned in Matthew 23:23.

Essentially the Scribes and Pharisees put their faith in following their rules and not in God. The word "Pharisee," means separated. Their burning desire was to separate themselves from those who did not observe the laws of ritual purity and tithing and other matters they considered very important. While these matters may have been something that should not have been ignored, it was the condescending, arrogant attitude of the Scribes and Pharisees toward others that Jesus detested. It was for that reason that Christ bravely spoke against them when He said in Matthew 23:28, "So you, too, outwardly appear righteous to men, but inwardly you are full of hypocrisy and lawlessness."

The devil does not want us to ever be free from a dependence on performing rituals as a test of holiness. He knows well that his bullet of self-righteousness will never be fired if God's people were liberated from patterns that we have allowed to become objects of worship. Satan tries to convince us that if we alter our routines God will not be present or pleased. The devil wants us to operate out of a sense of guilt when we falter in our rituals. Ultimately, Satan would prefer that "devotion" be our god, not God be our devotion.

Let me share a personal example of how I faced this hellish trickery. When my children were very young, Annie and I began fasting and praying for them. We chose to commit each Wednesday to doing this. Though fasting is an incredibly wonderful regimen and has yielded significant results in our children's lives, there were times when I simply could not follow through on a particular Wednesday.

For example, I might go several weeks without missing a Wednesday, then visitors would show up or a business luncheon with a publisher or music business person might be scheduled on a Wednesday, and the day would be a loss in terms of fasting. When this happened there would be a very real sense of guilt and regret that nagged at my heart: "Well, you've failed your children. Shame on you. Your kids are going to suffer because you let them down this week. And God is really disappointed with you. Do you not love Him enough and the children He gave you to tell those folks that you cannot be with them on Wednesday?"

I learned early on that these accusations were not from God. They were the devil's attempt to make me put my trust in the process and not in the Lord. I had to resist the feelings of regret and shame regarding missed Wednesdays. I had to learn to be flexible and trust that God's grace extended well beyond my occasional faltering when it came to the regimen I wanted to follow.

I challenge us to become what Jesus was during the time He physically walked on the earth. While He was not a sinner, He was definitely a "religious rule breaker." Not only did He often verbally square off with the Scribes and Pharisees, He openly associated with sinners like Zacchaeus (Luke 19), and He spoke kindly to women (John 4). In addition He made strange and shocking statements such as "But whoever wishes to be first among you shall be your slave" (Matthew 20:26). His willingness to break from the traditions of man and their ritualistic mind-set of the times made it very difficult to pigeonhole the Savior. It certainly frustrated the religious leaders of the day and they became His greatest enemies.

If you dodge the bullet of self-righteousness by forsaking a "vain repetition" you have held in too high esteem, you may encounter a new enemy. It could very well be someone near you who possesses the accusing spirit of the Scribes and Pharisees. But let his or her unmerited judgment be a cause for joy because it will be a sign that you have successfully dethroned the god of ritualism.

There's one other important consideration when it comes to avoiding the danger of being patterned. Perhaps for some men the most challenging part of forsaking the god of a treasured ritual is to be willing to accept something that a lot of guys, myself included, try to avoid like an irritated skunk. That dreadful thing is…change.

I'm convinced that men are more like God than women

because we can be "the same yesterday, today, and forever." Many of us simply do not like to change. But without a willingness to break the rules, we run the risk of walking into the sight path of the enemy's gun barrel. It may be hard to embrace the challenge of change, but our spiritual longevity could be at stake. When I struggle with resisting change, all I need to do is recall the sudden report of Lindsey's 12-gauge on the afternoon of the memorable turkey hunt. The echo of the blast reminds me that an easy target makes an easy kill. I don't want to be an easy mark for the hunter from hell.

Do you know you are under surveillance? Perhaps you've never considered that your steps are being watched and that your precious routines are of major interest to the enemy of your soul. One thing is certain, if you keep entering the woods of your spiritual life everyday in the same exact place because you believe therein is righteousness, sooner or later your feathers are gonna fly.

> They watch my steps, as they have
> waited to take my life.
> PSALM 56:6

9

Laid Bare

It was an October day early in archery season and I was at home. Annie was in our bedroom changing and bathing our nine-month-old granddaughter, who had filled her little britches with "baby paste." When Annie returned to our den she handed Lily Anne to me. As I held her I volunteered an admission.

"Babe, it's a funny thing. I gag at even the thought of changing this youngin's dirty diaper, but I can gut a freshly killed deer and eat a sandwich at the same time. Go figure!"

Annie laughed and said, "You need help, Honey!"

"I suppose," I agreed, "but I don't know what it is about my psyche that can let me open up a whitetail from its groin to its sternum without a hint of nausea, but I'm afraid I'll faint if I have to pull the tabs on one of those poop pockets that little Miss Lily is wearing."

"Sooner or later you're gonna have to do it, Steve."

"I'll take later if you don't mind."

During that deer season I also encountered another quirky trait about me that has to do with field dressing a deer. It happened while Annie and I were watching TV. She had the remote (the story of my life) and was flipping through the channels on our set. Suddenly she landed on the Discovery channel and stopped. I nearly ran out of the room at the sight that filled our 21-inch screen, but Annie leaned forward in her chair signifying that the images had her undivided attention. I begged her to move on to another channel. Instead she just glanced at me with that "You'll have to pry this remote out of my cold, dead fingers" expression, smiled maniacally, and looked back at the TV. I bowed my head, buried my face in my hands, and said, "Just tell me when it's over."

Curiosity got the best of me so I cautiously looked back at the TV. There on the screen was a close-up shot of a doctor's scalpel slicing through the chest cavity of some poor soul. I couldn't help but wonder if the guy even knew that the carnage they were rendering to his body was being recorded. I could feel my entire face pucker in horror as I groaned in sympathy.

Annie looked over at me and said, "The great hunter, slayer, and butcher of beasts can't take it!"

She was right, but I had to offer my best defense for my weakness. "You know, Babe, doing that to an animal is one thing, but watching one of my own getting field dressed is downright painful."

"Well, I'd like to see this if you don't mind."

"Okay, but bless that feller's heart," I mumbled and assumed that was exactly what the doctors were intending to do.

As the razor sharp blade cut through the numbed epidermis of the unfortunate humanoid on the table, blood oozed from the intentional wound. I wondered how on earth the surgeon could sound so nonchalant as he spoke to the camera about what he was doing. If I were him I would have been screaming, "I'm so sorry, Sir. Please forgive me. Call a doctor! Somebody please call 911!"

I groaned again at the sight of the surgeon's bloody, gloved hands as they worked their woe. Once again I pleaded with Annie to go on to something else. I conjured up a cry in my voice and said, "I'll settle for a ballet, a cooking show, Martha, ice skating, reruns of our town counsel meeting, anything." But she gripped the remote a little tighter, pursed her lips, and said, "Look at that! They cut the fellow from his belly button to his neck. Imagine that. And we're getting to watch the whole thing." At that, I went outside and shot a few arrows at my foam block. I couldn't take the reality of the operation...or was it a murder? I wasn't sure.

Later on that evening Annie explained her fascination with the Discovery channel show we (she) watched that day. She said, "The reason I found the video so interesting is that when I saw the doctor opening up his patient, I thought of a passage of Scripture I had been thinking about the last couple of days."

I took the opportunity that was put before me. "It wouldn't be the one in Acts that says, 'and falling headlong, he burst open in the middle and all his entrails gushed out,' would it?"

She managed a courtesy chuckle and said, "Good guess, but not quite. Let me get my Bible and I'll read it to you." What she proceeded to tell me truly was a remarkable insight into a passage that has since taken on a new meaning, especially as a hunter.

She said, "The passage is Hebrews 4:12 and 13. It reads, 'For the word of God is living and active and sharper than any two-edged sword, and piercing as far as the division of soul and spirit, of both joints and marrow, and able to judge the thoughts and intentions of the heart. And there is no creature hidden from His sight, but all things are open and laid bare to the eyes of Him with whom we have to do.'"

When she finished the pair of verses she looked up, pulled her glasses off and asked, "Did you hear what I see?"

I stood there in the kitchen, holding a cup of coffee, hardly able to wait to hear how my darling wife had connected the Hebrews passage to the bloody sights we had seen. She explained, "A two-edged sword was designed to cut through metal armor. It is a picture of how deep the Word of God can probe into the spirit of someone. It can judge even the thoughts and intentions that a person tries to hide. That in itself is an amazing thought, but what I saw today on TV was someone being 'laid bare.' That doctor was opening that guy up like a Christmas turkey, laying him bare so that all things would be open to his physician eyes."

Annie could tell she had my attention. A woman can often tell if her husband is engaged in what she is saying by whether or not he is looking at her when she talks. I was all eyes as Annie continued.

"The doctor wasn't cutting his patient open because he was being mean to him. No, he split that fellow in two because his intentions were to help a sick man. Something was wrong with his patient, and the doctor opened him up to see what it was. You weren't in the room when the doctor visually probed around the guy's open chest and said, 'There's the problem.' Then he proceeded to fix it."

"You watched the whole show?" I was amazed when she admitted she endured every stitch.

"I did," she announced and continued, "and it was a great

picture of what God does for those of us who are spiritually sick. His Word is a sharp scalpel. With it He lays us bare, not because He wants to be mean to us, but because He loves us enough to do the surgery. Once we're laid bare in His presence He can say, 'O, there's that greed that's making him sick' or 'There's that disease of envy that has plagued her for so long.' For others he might say, 'O, there's that addiction to pornography, food, alcohol, pills.' All this can happen when our hearts are open before Him."

Being an avid student of the Scriptures, Annie's eyes always gleam when she finds new pictures she can use to help others understand biblical truth. She had that sparkle as she continued. "Before I would ever get on an operating table and submit to a surgeon's knife, I sure would want to know that he had plenty of experience and that he could be trusted. Getting references is a smart thing to do when you're looking for a trustworthy doctor. And when it comes to God, the Great Physician, if someone were to ask me about Him, I would take them to the woman caught in the act of adultery in John 8. She could testify to the Lord's forgiveness and to how His words, 'From now on sin no more,' cut through to the very center of her heart. I'd take them to the woman at the well in John 4. She could tell how Jesus laid her bare with, 'You have correctly said, "I have no husband"; for you have had five husbands, and the one whom you now have is not your husband…' I'd take them to Zaccheus in Luke 19, and let them hear his report about how Christ can look inside a person, see his sin-sick soul and slice through his sinful nature with kind words like, 'Today I must stay at your house.'"

And then Annie said, "If they'd ask me, I could gladly tell

them that God is good at what He does. I could give Him a really good referral."

That last statement was loaded with Annie's firsthand knowledge that God indeed can be trusted to lay any of us bare and repair any part of us that may be sick. When she has the opportunity to give her personal testimony of how God used His written Word to lay her heart bare before Him, she knows of the divine skill and mercy of which she speaks. It was not until she submitted to the sharp blade of God's truth that He cut through to the very core of her being and exposed the sickening effects of the rape she experienced when she was a child. The infection existed in the forms of anger, fear, hatred, and unforgiveness. But God, in His great mercy, performed His miracle operation in Annie's life. When he laid her heart bare with His Word, He was able to repair her. So without question her desire to help others know that the Lord is an experienced Healer is born out of having been His patient.

As we sat at the table that evening, Annie told me a story that provides a very clear picture of how the Word of God can cut through even the hardest exterior of a person. In the case of the lady she told me about, her "emotional skin" had been hardened by hatred and pride. Only the razor sharp edge of God's Word could make the necessary incision that led to her healing. Sadly, her situation involved a falling out with her sibling.

"There is a woman I know," Annie began, "whose brother said something to her that she deeply resented. In fact, her brother cursed at her as he was saying it, and she didn't feel she deserved his ranting. She decided she would never speak to him again. The problem was, she went to her other two siblings and told them what he had done. Unfortunately, the woman's siblings told too many people, and somehow it got back to the brother that she had exposed his vulgar comments. Well, at first she couldn't have cared less about how he felt and was content to never pick up the phone and call him or go to his house…until one day when she was reading the book of Proverbs. Two passages got her attention."

Annie opened her Bible to the passages and read them to me. "In Proverbs 10:12 the offended sister found, 'Hatred stirs up strife, but love covers all transgressions.' Then she read the verse in 18:19 that says, 'A brother offended is harder to be won than a strong city.'"

Annie continued, "What made these two verses leap out at this woman was the fact that she is a Christian, and she had always hoped to win her brother to Christ. Yet her anger toward him was so fierce that she had forsaken any attempt to talk to him about it. But when she read the verses in Proverbs, the Word laid her heart bare. She wept as she realized that by allowing her tongue to stir up strife she had possibly done greater damage to his life than his cursing had done to hers. She was tortured by the fear that her brother might never be open to the gospel because of her actions."

I was hoping there was a happy ending to the story so I asked, "And what did she do once the Word had exposed her bitterness toward her brother?"

"With her heart laid bare before the Lord, He was able to identify the spiritual and emotional infection that was making her sick. First she confessed her sin of creating trouble in her family to the Lord, and then she went to her brother and asked him to forgive her for what she had done to him. She said later that it was without a doubt one of the most painful things she had ever done, but yet it yielded such an enormous amount of peace. She said she hated being sick with hatred, but the good news is, as sick as she was with it, that's how good she felt when the pride had been removed. But the kind of healing she needed would have never happened if the Scriptures had not laid her heart bare before the Lord."

Annie looked toward the TV and said, "Now you know why I was so glued to that show today. As gross as such an operation is for viewers to watch, imagine what the Lord thinks when He opens us up and sees the deadly spiritual infections such as puss of pride, or cancer of gossip, or the tumors of lust in our spirits. May God help us all."

As I began to wonder what God would find if he suddenly laid me bare, Annie added one more statement: "I hope the next time you sharpen your knife and get ready to gut a deer you'll think of the words 'laid bare' in Hebrews 4."

My response was what she expected. "You know, there may be a study on Hebrews happening tomorrow morning… it starts really early, before daylight, and I think I should go!"

Annie smiled and then she gave me some instructions that made me really nervous. "If you go hunting in the morning, don't forget that Heidi is bringing Lily over tomorrow. We need you to be back from the woods by 11 so you can watch her all afternoon while we go to town. Heidi said she'd bring plenty of diapers!"

10

Dream Coming True

The sound of the two huge jet engines just outside the fuselage walls began to grow to a deafening roar as the airliner began its roll down the runway. Seat 21-B was not the best seat in the flying house, but it was the one I was assigned.

The feeling of apprehension about the inherent safety risks that flying can have was plenty to worry about. However, something else was bothering me on that predawn departure from Nashville, Tennessee. I knew that it was the opening day of archery deer season, and it was killing me that I couldn't be in the stand that morning.

My absence from the woods was made doubly painful by lifting off the runway and looking easterly at the sky that was beginning to lighten. The pale, grayish-blue horizon was clear—not a cloud in sight. The air temperature was just crisp enough to not only keep the mosquitoes in their beds for an extra hour or two that morning but cold enough to keep the deer active for a little longer than normal. I was well aware that I was missing what would surely be one of the most glorious openings of a season that I would ever have experienced as a hunter. I was truly bummed.

Why had this fate come to me? What could have possibly

been more important than slipping quietly into the ladder stand I had gone to so much trouble to set up? The answer is almost embarrassing to reveal because when you realize why I couldn't go hunting, you're not going to feel sorry for me. But I'll tell you anyway.

That morning I was flying to a city to be the keynote speaker at an event called a Wild Game Dinner. My prescribed duty was to, get this, talk and sing for an hour or so about hunting! That's right. I had the grand privilege of being the designated presenter to a crowd of like-minded hunters who would be coming to a building graced with appropriate decorations such as camo cloth, buck, bear, and bass mounts, touches of blaze orange, and probably some strategically placed foliage that would make them all feel like they were outdoors inside.

In addition, as the attendees entered the dining hall the inviting odor of the skillfully prepared wild game dishes would likely make their every breath an aromatic treat, causing their saliva glands to kick into overdrive. Then during the event there would be a plethora of exciting and well-chosen door prizes that would make each attendee happily tense with hope each time a winning number would be plucked out of the bucket of names.

Like I said, that's where I was heading. And now that you know, you probably are rolling your eyes and saying, "It's a dirty job, but somebody's gotta do it!" I can't say that I blame you. I shouldn't have felt such sorrow for myself that morning, yet I did.

Because of the kind of work I do, I frequently travel Friday through Monday. Consequently, I often have to miss the first day of most seasons. Whether it is deer, turkey, bear, rabbit, or squirrel, you name the season, I've missed the opening day of it. The one thing that can get me through a weekend of a lost opener is knowing that if the Lord wills, when Monday comes I'll get to put on my camo duds and feed the hunger for the hunt that has gnawed at me since the previous season closed.

In the past few years, whenever I miss an opening day, I can't help but think of those who are in places where they will not only miss the first morning, but they'll have to forego the entire season. For some, their absence might be temporary, but still it's a tough reality to deal with. For example, there are soldiers who are deployed around the world who may be thousands of miles from the familiar homeland mountains and meadows that they would love to be walking when a season comes in. Instead they're on strange soil, not hunting, but being hunted. But while they proudly wear the uniform of their branch of service, they probably dream of wearing the uniform of the hunter again. And though they may miss a season, maybe two or even three, they are consoled by the thought that at least there will come a day when hopefully they will get to enjoy their investment in the freedoms they protect, especially the freedom to hunt.

While I ache for the hunters who are soldiers, there is another type of person whose absence from the woods is far more painful for me to think about. That hunter is high-lighted in this song lyric.

Dream Coming True

Slower than a shadow on a sundial
He moves to get his fingers on the string
He prays that the wind won't turn the other way
'Cause it's the biggest whitetail he has ever seen

Another Look at Life from a Deer Stand

And the morning golden sun lights up the antlers
But he knows he can't let them steal his mind
So he picks a spot of fur behind the shoulder
And he whispers, "Ten more yards, and boy, you're mine!"

He's got a dream coming true
He's been living in the moment for so long
October sun
Up on that mountain
He's up there in that stand all alone
There ain't nothing else he'd rather do
He's got a dream coming true

Well the white oak trees
Are raining down their candy
So that old whitetail
He's got his eyes to the ground
Seconds seem like years
As he moves into the lane
The hunter begs his trembling arms
"Don't fail me now."

The moment pounds his heart
Like a hammer
And as the arrow flies
He hears that prison guard
He knows it's time to go back
To his cell inside the walls
But he pleads for one more minute
In the yard…'cause

He's got a dream coming true
He's been living in this moment
For so long
October sun

Up on that mountain
He's up there in that stand
All alone
There ain't nothing else
He'd rather do
He's got a dream coming true
All he has is a dream
Coming true[1]

I have tried to imagine what it would be like to go from
being completely free to head to the woods to being completely denied the joy. To be honest, I can't dwell on even the
thought of such a sad thing for very long without feeling a
depth of sorrow that brings me to near tears. I'm afraid it
would yield more depression than I could possibly handle.
Yet year after year, season after season, there are those who
can only dream of the hunt and hope that someday, somehow
they'll be able to feel the reality of it again.

Since the release of the few books I've penned about my
love for the outdoors, I have been privileged to receive a good
number of letters from prisoners who have read them. I'm
not sure how the books get into their hands, but I assume that
in many cases they are sent by caring family members whose
intent is to provide a connection to something their loved one
enjoyed before incarceration. Perhaps friends send them for
the same reason. But in whatever way they get the books, I am
grateful that they are seen as worthwhile gifts to individuals
whose place in life leaves them so far away from the deer
stand. And, I suppose it is intense sympathy that I feel for the
locked away hunters that drives me as much as anything else
to correspond with them.

One of the most memorable letters that came in the mail

from an inmate was sent to me from an individual I mentioned in the devotional for deer hunters called *With God on a Deer Hunt*. His letter included not only a nice note about one of my other books he had read but also a song lyric. When I read the verses and chorus and realized who had actually written the words, I was deeply touched by them. The writer was a gentleman named James Alley. As you read his lyric, think about the environment in which he wrote it.

He Never Did Anything

There's an angry crowd
Outside the city walls
And they're cursing at a man
Hanging on a cross
They're saying to Him, "Save yourself
If You're a king!"
But He was blameless as a lamb

He never did anything
He never did anything
But come to save the lost
He never did anything
But pay the final cost
He healed the sick, raised the dead
And took away the sting
But when it came to finding fault in Him
He never did anything

When there's an angry storm
That grows inside of me
I put my trust in the One
Who calmed the angry sea

And when I'm lonely
He makes my sad heart sing
How could they ever crucify Him
He never did anything[2]

I have continually prayed for the day James gets his day in court. But until then, I was blessed to have been able to provide him with a spark of delight. I took his lyric, set it to music, recorded it onto a cassette and sent it to him. Not only did he receive the tape but I also included a letter asking him for permission to record the song on a CD project that Annie and I completed called *This House Still Stands.*

Not too many days after we sent him the final mix of the song, I received a letter from him. In it was one of the most moving statements I could have ever imagined getting in the mail. He said, "Before the tape came I looked in the mirror and all I saw was a prisoner. Today when I look in the mirror, I see a songwriter."

I have held on to his words like an old gold miner would clutch a knuckle-sized nugget. To put it in deer hunter's terms, there is no set of antlers anywhere that can outsize the trophy that James hung on the wall of my heart.

Without a retrial that would result in a reduced sentence or even an acquittal, James has several years ahead of him to serve before his debt of time is paid in full. As each year passes, another entire deer season will go by without James being there to walk the woods of his home state of Ohio. He can only dream about it. To say the very least, that puts things in perspective for me.

Let the groaning of the prisoner come before You.
PSALM 79:11

11

Turtle on a Fence Post

I dismounted my ladder stand around ten in the morning on a warm, late-September day and headed home. As I walked the fence row that would lead me back to my pickup, I nearly stepped on one of God's most interesting creatures. It was a turtle. It's head and short legs were protruding when I saw it, but when it saw me it instantly pulled all of its appendages inside the shell and closed the hatch doors.

I was standing next to a wooden fence post that supported the barbed wire that was tightly strung, and I leaned my bow against the lower of the four strands. Then I gently gathered up the turtle and held it at eye level to make sure that the hard shell was completely closed. After determining that the creature was well tucked away I carefully set it on the flat top of the post. I placed the turtle there for a good reason. I wanted to see a real live version of a word picture my son had painted in my mind only a few weeks prior to that September day.

Nathan is a full-grown man now, standing well above me at a height of nearly six feet, four. It's hard to believe he was once the little guy whose legs barely reached the edge of the couch as we sat together and belly laughed at Bugs Bunny and

Daffy Duck. And it's especially hard to believe that the adolescent I gave my tired and overused instruments and recording equipment to years ago is now using the experience gained from those gifts as the foundation on which he has built a business of making and producing music. In fact, most of the recordings that Annie and I offer today have been produced by Nathan.

One day as Annie and I shared a lunch with our son, he began thanking us for all the hand-me-down items that he recalled getting at home. Repeating a quip he'd heard someone say, he smiled and humbly said, "At the time I didn't know what you meant when you said you'd rather give me tools than toys, but I understand it now." He also added, "I know that what I'm able to do today as a vocation, I wouldn't be doing if you and a lot of other folks had not provided the way." Then he said the words I thought of when I found the turtle. He said, "To be honest, I feel like a turtle on a fence post." We asked him to explain what he meant. His insight was heartwarming.

"As everyone knows, there's only one way a turtle can get on a fence post. Someone has to help it get up there. There's no way he can do it by himself. And that's the way I feel. I am where I am in life today because of the help of others, and it's a long list of names. I'd have to have a lot of paper and ink if I started writing down all the people who have helped make it possible for me to devote my full time to something I enjoy so much. I don't have time to mention all the names I've thought of, but suffice it to say that I am well aware that I needed the help. I will be forever grateful for all who have given it."

We were curious to hear some of the names, so we asked him to humor us and give us at least a few on his list. He didn't start with the two of us. Instead he said the name we wanted to hear most. "Of course," he began, "at the top of the list would be the Lord Jesus. I'm not being patronizing and proper in the presence of my Christian parents by saying His name. I put Him first with all sincerity. But I will say that after Him, you're next," and he looked at the two of us. We were never so happy for being in second place.

Then for several minutes he brought up very familiar family members such as his wife, Stephanie, his sister, Heidi, his grandparents, PJ and Lillian Chapman and N.R. and Sylvia Williamson. Then there were uncles and aunts, some cousins, and even a second cousin or two. He also included several of our older friends, some of his younger friends, church family, publishers, music teachers, high school and college teachers, roommates in college, and the names kept coming. We were astounded at the number of individuals that were on the tip of his tongue. He said, "I'm sure I've missed some, but it's amazing to think that it took all those folks to lift one young turtle."

Nathan's obvious appreciation inspired us to consider our own list of those who have lifted us up and set us on the fence post of opportunity. We too would start with recognizing God's boundless gifts to us. We would be ungrateful fools to overlook Him. After acknowledging the Lord, then we would mention our parents who placed so much of their lives into ours. Then, without question, our children would be next on the list simply because they invested so many years with us dealing with the rigors of the road. They traveled with us from colic to college and literally have done as much as anyone to help us fulfill the calling we sensed on our lives as itinerate musicians. Then we would add our siblings, friends, church associates, business partners, and on and on the list would grow. I do believe that Annie and I could fill a massive book with all the names and what each one contributed to these two turtles on a fence post. The higher the stack of names, the deeper the gratitude would be for all of them.

While I know I may risk offending someone by highlighting one specific person who would be on our list, I'd like to do so just to make a single important point. (If you're a deer hunter, you know "points" are important!) That point is that very often we may be lifting someone up on a fence post, and we don't even know it is happening at the time. It may not be until much later, even years later, that our name is added to someone's list of significant influencers. Such is the case for the one I personally want to mention. The huge difference this person made in my life didn't dawn on me until I was well into my career as a worker with words.

This particular individual may very well be the oldest living member at present on the list. And keep in mind, though she has affected both Annie's life and mine, her first influence was particularly on me. Her impact happened back when I was a young twelfth grader in high school. Her name is Mrs. Margaret Withrow.

In the 1960s, the name Mrs. Withrow generated a lot of sober respect in the minds of the students at Point Pleasant High School. If the new year came and a student was handed a list of the teachers they would be required to sit under that year, and if her name was on it, there was only one thing to do. The student would bow his head and ask for the Rapture of the Saints to happen during the prayer. That's what I did, but the Rapture didn't happen. Consequently, I would have to remain on earth and attend Mrs. Withrow's class.

I accepted my fate that my senior English course would be taught by the teacher who had the reputation for cracking the academic whip. I braced myself for failure. However, before the first bell sounded, I decided to take one more look at the class assignment form they had given me just to make sure I had read it correctly. What I discovered was some gloriously wonderful news. I noticed that it was not English that I would be taking from Mrs. Withrow. Instead, the assignment sheet said "Creative Writing." I didn't really know what it meant exactly, but at least it didn't say "English." I was ecstatic.

Well, it didn't take but about ten minutes in the first day of class to realize my grade average was still in jeopardy. Mrs. Withrow was standing up front using words I didn't know existed. As the next few days went on, I tried to hang on to her instructions but the fingers of learning were slipping off the cliff of hope. What's worse, the words she wrote on the chalkboard that I assumed had meaning in some language somewhere, were the very words she was asking us to use in sentences. And when we completed the sentences and strung them together, they were supposed to make sense. I was about to go ahead and let go of the rock of education that I was clinging to when something happened that changed my mind.

Just before the bell rang that signaled we could run out into the halls and scream in frustration, Mrs. Withrow said to the class, "Tomorrow, I want all of you to come with a poem. Be prepared to read it to the class. You're dismissed."

A poem, I thought as I gathered up my books and headed to the door. *Wow…now that sounds interesting. Four, maybe eight lines ought to do it. This should be easy. Cool!*

Like I was prone to do, I totally forgot about my homework until about 11 o'clock that night. In a panic I started wracking my tired brain for a theme for what I hoped would be the shortest poem on the planet. As I perused my thoughts I remembered a *Reader's Digest* article I had read just a few days earlier. It was about an American soldier fighting the war in Vietnam. He had received a copy of the Bible from his mother and put it into his shirt pocket the day it came in the mail. Within a short time his division came under fire, and the soldier was thrown to the ground by the impact of a bullet. He discovered that the bullet had hit him in his shirt pocket, and the Bible that his mother had sent stopped the projectile from piercing through his chest. He opened the Bible to dig the bullet out and found that the tip of the slug stopped at a specific page in the book of Psalms. The passage that the tip of the bullet was pointing to was Psalm 91:7: "A thousand shall fall at thy side, and ten thousand at thy right hand; but it shall not come nigh thee" (KJV).

I decided to try to capture this story in a poem. Little did I know that it would be one of the most enjoyable 60 minutes I would ever spend doing homework. When the last word was written I was thrilled that the poem had grown to 24 lines. It was a piece I called "Psalm 91:7."

That night, as I closed my spiral notebook and started to head to bed, an idea came to me that kept me up for another hour or two. I was a greenhorn guitar player at the time and knew a few chords. I thought to myself, *I wonder if Mrs. Withrow would let me sing this poem tomorrow instead of reading it?*

I uncased the Gibson J-45 and began strumming, looking for a melody. For some reason the music theme for the TV show *Gilligan's Island* kept running through my head. I figured, "Why not. It's easy and it'll be quick." So that was the chord pattern I based the song on and before long I had myself a real live, singable song.

I'll never forget how nervous I was when it came my turn to present my poem in the classroom the next day. My knees knocked like a badly tuned car engine as I approached the front. I strapped on my Gibson and about halfway through the song I realized that everyone in the room was actually listening.

When I finished, Mrs. Withrow promptly stood up, marched to the front, pinched my shirt sleeve in her fingers, and said as she pulled on me to follow her, "Come with me, Steve."

"Where are we going?"

"Just bring your poem and your guitar and come with me," she demanded.

I thought maybe I had transgressed some school policy and that I was headed to the principal's office to receive my sentence. I was sure I was about to join the rest of the punished souls who paid their debt by cleaning the bathrooms after school. Little did I know that instead of taking me to see Mr. Chambers, Mrs. Withrow was taking me to Mrs. Jackson's senior English class.

Unannounced, we barged into the room and Mrs. Withrow said, "Mrs. Jackson, whatever you're doing, could you stop for a minute and listen to something?"

"Certainly, Mrs. Withrow. What do you have for us?"

I was escorted to the center front of the room and told, "Now sing, young man." So, I sang the song again.

After I finished I was taken back to my Creative Writing classroom, and the rest is a blur. The only other thing I remember was something Mrs. Withrow said after we got back to the classroom. She took the piece of paper my verses were on and wrote across the top, "51...out of a possible 50!"

I couldn't believe my eyes. What she said to me as she stood at my desk has stayed with me through all my years. "Steve, you need to pursue the art of songwriting. I believe you have a knack for it. I gave you that score to show you how serious I am about this suggestion."

Basically, what Mrs. Withrow did in that moment was picked up a fragile, little helpless turtle and set it on the fence post of a vision. I don't think I would have gotten there if she had not been so kind to me that day. And the amazing thing is, there was no way she could know the long-term impact her encouragement had on my life. She was just doing her job as a teacher.

The next time you're out deer hunting or wandering around in the great outdoors, if you find a turtle, I hope you'll pick it up and think of two things. One, may you take the time to list all who have helped you do what you do, and two, the next time you get an opportunity to help someone in some way, may you remember that someday your name might show up on his or her list.

Psalm 91:7

A soldier o'er in Vietnam
Got a package clear from home
In it a Bible marked, "Love, your Mom...
Read it wherever you roam."

Well he placed it in his khaki shirt
Just in front of his trembling heart
Then all of the sudden he hit the dirt
A bullet had hit him hard

He lay there on the ground a while
Just wondering what to do
Not a doc within a mile
He figured he was through

Then all of the sudden a smile appeared
As he raised his precious head
The bullet through the Bible had pierced
And he knew that he was far from dead

He took the little black book out
And the bullet stopped at page one eleven
He began to read aloud
Psalm 91:7

"A thousand shall fall at thy knee
And ten thousand at thy right hand
But it shall not come nigh to thee
Till you reach that promised land"

Then a praise swelled up within his heart
As tears came in his eyes
From my mother's prayers I'll never part
Till we meet there in the skies[1]

12

First-Time Caller

If you were to ask me or any other serious deer hunter to tell one of our favorite hunting memories, you should be warned that our story might require more of your time than you want to give. Plus, we would struggle with choosing just one memory due to the fact that they are a little like our children in that we love them all and think each one is incredible. So what's my favorite story? I told a very brief version of the account in my devotional book *With God on a Deer Hunt*, but I have looked forward to revealing the memorable details of this particular hunt for quite some time.

The old logging road on the 400-acre farm I was hunting ran straight along a ridgeline for quite a distance and then made a wide, sweeping turn through the woods. On one side of the road was a steep slope that dropped off the ridge down to a water source. I placed my climbing stand on the opposite side, about 60 yards off the road in the open timber, because very often I would watch deer come up out of the ravine and get onto the logging road that was lined with huge white oak trees. Usually they would feed along the 100 yards or so where the acorns had dropped onto the road, and then they'd make a right turn into the woods and walk through the area where I was set up. They favored that route because if they followed the ridgeline, it led them downhill into a bottom where a heavy thicket provided plenty of cover for them to bed down for the day.

When ten o'clock in the morning arrived, I had not seen a sign of fur. I was about to start my dismount from the tree when movement caught my eye to the left. Suddenly, I saw one lone, antlered deer step onto the logging road and casually began enjoying a midmorning feast of freshly fallen acorns. Thankful that I had no particular deadlines to meet, and that I could stay put for the excitement, I slowly stood to my feet and prepared for a possible close-up encounter of what looked to be a nice Tennessee buck.

Though it probably took only a few minutes for the deer to meander to the place on the logging road where they usually turned right and walked by my treestand placement, it seemed like an hour. Finally the buck was within 20 yards of the trail, and my pulse was at a level that would test even the strongest heart.

Though he was at least 45 yards away I had no trouble seeing the deer's form through the mature stand of timber. However, what I couldn't see was inside the animal's mind. There was no way I could have predicted that he would choose to ignore the trail that followed the ridge where I sat and instead would walk right on by. I couldn't believe it! My disappointed heart sank through my nervous gut. All I could do was watch him follow the wide sweep of the road that would lead him to the backside of the farm. But then I remembered something I had with me that I thought might save the day.

The only problem was I felt a little doubtful about my ability to put it into action.

I had never used a grunt call in all my years of whitetail hunting. I purchased the one I had with me some time before that day and had practiced at home with the instructional cassette tape that came with the device, but I had not put it to the test in the real woods. I knew my calling ability was questionable at best. I figured it was time to give it a try.

I searched for the small metal zipper tab on my jacket. I quietly pulled down on the zipper, slid my hand inside and felt around for the tube that hung around my neck at the end of a short lanyard. When I found it, I put my fingers around it and paused for a couple of seconds to process my thoughts.

To start with, I was dealing with the doubts I had about actually trying to "talk" to a deer for the first time. After all, the whitetail and I are different. Someone said about God and man that we're different not in degree, but in kind. The same is true for man and deer. Though we're each made of flesh and blood and both of us have an instinct for survival, for the most part we are two totally and completely different creatures that were not designed for vocally communicating with each other. Yet in my hand I held a potential link between my mind and his. However, I knew if I produced the wrong sound the buck's quick departure would be likely.

Though I felt a little anxious about proceeding, any reservations I was feeling were quickly cast aside because the buck was getting away! In the few seconds I spent arguing with myself, he had walked on around the bend of the road and turned left, entered the timber, and was about to casually stroll out of sight. My window of opportunity was closing! I had nothing to lose but a bucketful of ego so I mentally rehearsed the sound I had heard on the demo tape and put the call to my mouth.

Though he was out of range for my arrow I didn't think he was out of earshot for the sound of the call. With the open end of the tube pointed toward the buck I gently forced some air through the mouthpiece of the call. The best way to describe the short, guttural sound the device made was that it resembled a man's post-meal burp. It's actually not a lovely sound, at least to the nonhunter's ear. To me the grunt sounded like sweet music.

I was surprised at how much the call favored the demonstrations I had listened to on the tape. I was duly impressed with the sound I had made, but I was much more excited by what I saw immediately after the call went forth. The walking deer stopped dead in his tracks and looked my way. Though I had no idea what I had just said to him, I was hoping his interpretation of my call was, "I'm one of you. Come back here!"

As if he had thought it through and decided his ears were playing tricks on him, he started to walk away again. When he did I quickly put the call to my mouth once more and blew just a little bit louder. He stopped again and slightly turned his head toward me. I couldn't see his face clearly, but I imagined it had an expression that might have said, "That sure did sound like another deer. Nah…it couldn't be." And then he walked on again.

When he took a couple of more steps I realized one more try would probably be the last hurrah for my first attempt to communicate with a deer. With that possibility in mind, I cast aside all inhibition, put the call to my lips, and gave it a rather forceful, louder, longer, and more confident burst of air. I still wasn't sure what the call would say to the buck, but what I wanted him to hear this time was "I'm here to steal your girlfriend, Bubba!"

The call must have sounded like some sort of threat because the thrill of what happened next made me nearly fall out of my stand. He stopped and abruptly turned his head precisely in my direction and gave an aggressive looking stare. Though I was sure he couldn't see me among the foliage it appeared he knew exactly where the source of the sound was located. Thankfully the slight breeze was coming from him to me so I knew if he decided to check me out the conditions were in my favor.

For about three or four seconds that seemed like minutes he looked behind himself then suddenly he wheeled around on his back hooves and began walking toward my stand. My legs shook with excitement as I replaced the tube in my jacket and zipped it up to make sure that if I got a shot the string wouldn't catch on it.

When he crossed back over the logging road and entered the section of the woods where I was, he was on a brisk, deliberate pace. As he walked his head went side to side like radar, obviously looking to find the challenging intruder. He didn't look downward to the ground as he came so I knew I would have to wait for the moment his eyes would go behind a huge oak that stood between us about 20 yards out. I instantly calculated that the angle he would walk as he went by the tree would provide about two seconds for me to get to full draw. It would be my only chance to not be detected by his very keen eyes.

When he reached the oak I put every ounce of strength I could muster into getting to full draw. My overly excited arm muscles trembled pitifully as I pulled back on the taut string.

Thankfully the arrow did not jump out of the two-pronged rest. Finally the peep sight was at my eye, and I quickly found fur in the opening.

With about ten more yards to cover before he would step into range of my bow, I fought the sweat that trickled into my right eye. Knowing very well that I couldn't complete a shot with blurred vision I had to do something fast. While still at full draw with my hand at my jaw I quickly abandoned the attempt to blink the sweat away, raised my hand to eye level and carefully raked my gloved thumb across my eyelash to absorb the salty water. It worked! Once again I could see clearly as I found the deer for the second time in the peep sight.

As the buck came closer I assumed he would walk right on by me. Thankfully, however, he suddenly came to an abrupt halt and stood broadside at a mere 12 yards from my stand. Somehow his incredible sense of hearing and his amazing ability to calculate the distance from his ear drums to sound source seemed to make him aware of exactly how far to walk. While he paused I put my 15 yard sight pin on the lower area of his vitals and slowly put pressure on the release trigger. The bow recoiled in my hands as the arrow began its short flight.

The slap of the bow limbs as they collapsed probably sounded like the blast of a gun shot in the quiet of the timber, but I didn't hear it. I also didn't hear the buck dig into the thick blanket of dried leaves as he made his explosive departure. All I knew in that instant was that the many things that must go right in order for a dream to become reality in the deer hunter's woods had done just that. Not only had I arrowed a nice Tennessee buck, it was the first time ever that I had managed to talk an animal into coming to me. The fatally wounded buck didn't run but 20 yards, staggered, and within mere seconds was transferred from nature's care to the responsibility of Grissoms Meats, my favorite local wild game processor, who would receive him later on that morning.

I stood there amazed that a simple combination of a little bit of breath passing through a plastic tube over a thin reed would yield such a result. Using my extremely limited whitetail vocabulary, I had spoken a language that a creature so vastly different than me had understood, believed, and accepted. My call had spanned the huge communication gap between animal and man.

To this day, what happened that morning several years ago remains one of the most unforgettable and treasured experiences because it represents such a monumental accomplishment for me as a deer hunter. But there is another reason I am so fond of the memory of this particular hunt. It's a picture of something that happened to me back in 1974, a life-changing event.

As the mid-1970s approached, I was, so to speak, alone in the woods of life. At that time I had wandered aimlessly into my twenties, doubtful of my purpose for existing. I had no direction and no vision for my future. As a young man coming out of the late 60s and entering the early 70s, my thinking had been seriously influenced by the social tone of the times. My generation found identity in having no identity. It was a time when nothing was wrong and everything was right. The rebellion against "the establishment" of our parents' conservative ways was signaled by several things.

For example, we let our "freak flags fly." That phrase was a line from a popular song of the times that, when interpreted, meant, "No, you can't make us cut our hair." We kept as few clothes as possible, mostly denim and flannel, and for the most part only what we could carry on our backs. And by all means, it was never cool to use a lot of soap. Just a little dab would do us. When it came to personal hygiene we believed in being as "natural" as possible. The problem in those days with being natural is the same problem it is now...natural stinks! There were plenty of products available on the market to do battle against the odors created by "natural," but it just didn't seem cool to use them.

My choice to partake in a lifestyle that I knew was considered unacceptable by those I loved and liked left me feeling uncomfortably disconnected from both family and friends. They certainly didn't disown me, but they did seem very reserved when I was around them. I couldn't see it then, but I now realize that the troubled expressions on the faces of my family when they saw me in my "hippieness" was not that of fear, but of cautious pity. Sadly, at that time I saw their desire to keep their distance as a form of rejection. Today I know they were struggling with what to say to someone whom they so deeply loved but who had so drastically changed. Their most serious concern was for the obvious fact that I had traded the narrow way of the Christian faith for the destructive, dark path of sin that the Scriptures call "the broad way."

A hesitance to embrace my errant state of heart was also visible in my long-time church friends. They scattered when I came around. The folks in the small town were simply not as open to my "far out" mindset as I thought they should be. But the disconnect I sensed because of the suspicious reactions of those who were once so close was not the worst of the feelings I faced in those times. I was in great turmoil in my spirit because I felt dangerously alienated from God. And it was that troubling realization that prevented me from fully enjoying the pleasures that were so easily accessible in the lifestyle of "loose living" I had chosen.

There is a name for the unsettled, uneasy feeling that gripped me whenever I dabbled in sin. Christians call it *conviction*. This term has its roots in John 8:7 in the story of the woman who was caught in the act of adultery. Jesus rescued her from being stoned by her accusers by challenging them with the well-known words, "He who is without sin among you, let him be the first to throw a stone at her." Verse nine in the New King James Version of the Bible reveals what happened next: "Then those who heard it, being *convicted* by their conscience, went out one by one."

With that scriptural account as the backdrop, "conviction" is often used by Christians to describe an awareness that rises up in an individual when they are in a spiritually unredeemed condition: "He or she has fallen under conviction." While the term can sound strange to those who have never heard it used in such a way, it is a very good description of the definite feeling of guilt that can gnaw at the soul. That's exactly what was happening in me.

The best comparison I can think of is that the conviction was like a blazing fire in my spirit that would not go out. It was a persistent fever, so to speak, that was warning me that something inside my soul was wrong. As hard as I tried, I could not dowse that intense fire of dread I felt in my heart. My desperate attempts to enjoy my waywardness simply didn't work.

There had been enough seed of the Scriptures sown in my heart by my parents as I grew up to produce the fruit of an understanding between right and wrong. While I walked the "broad road," there was an abiding fear of what eternity held for me if I died as a sinner. Try as I did, I could not make the uneasiness go away. What I didn't know was that the Divine Hunter, God Himself was nearby. He saw me wandering lost and lonely, feeling alienated from family and friends and walking farther away from Him each day. He lovingly called out to me.

Amazingly, God's call came from a place I least expected. Instead of coming from outside my heart, His call came from within the undying flames of fear that I had of being separated from Him. No, His voice was not audible. It came in the form of a very keen and quiet awareness in my heart that I desperately needed to turn around and go to Him. That inner call is explained in John 6:44 when Jesus said, "No one can come to Me unless the Father who sent Me draws him." God was indeed calling out to my heart.

In a way, the fire of conviction God spoke to my heart reminds me of what happened to Moses on the backside of the wilderness as recorded in the book of Exodus, chapter three. The account reads:

> Now Moses was pasturing the flock of Jethro his father-in-law, the priest of Midian; and he led the flock to the west side of the wilderness and came to Horeb, the mountain of God.
>
> The angel of the LORD appeared to him in a blazing fire from the midst of a bush; and he looked, and behold, the bush was burning with fire, yet the bush was not consumed.
>
> So Moses said, "I must turn aside now and see this marvelous sight, why the bush is not burned up."
>
> When the LORD saw that he turned aside to look, God called to him from the midst of the bush and said, "Moses, Moses!"

And he said, "Here I am."

Then He said, "Do not come near here; remove your sandals from your feet, for the place on which you are standing is holy ground."

He said also, "I am the God of your father, the God of Abraham, the God of Isaac, and the God of Jacob."

Then Moses hid his face, for he was afraid to look at God (Exodus 3:1-7).

Notice that it was in the moment when Moses said, "I must turn aside now and see this marvelous sight," that God spoke audibly to the man. The stunned shepherd surely was amazed and awed as God's voice came from *within* the burning bush saying, "Moses, Moses!" And the man could only answer with a trembling, "Here I am."

I can remember in early 1974 coming to grips with the fact that it was quite apparent that the fire of guilt in my spiritual bosom was not going to be extinguished. As frustrating as it was to sense the flames wouldn't diminish, I didn't know to be thankful that in reality it was the Holy Spirit of God who was calling me to turn to Christ. I readily admit that I was very irritated that the heat of guilt would not let me relax and enjoy the pleasures of sin. When I tried to disregard the fire, it burned hotter. All my attempts to kill the flames only fueled them. I tried dowsing the fire with mind-altering substances, unwholesome entertainment, and even surrounding myself with friends who shared my resistance to following God. Yet the conviction raged on.

Finally, in March of that year, I responded to God's call. To put it in hunter's terms, like the buck I called in with my grunt call, I stopped, wheeled around, and then headed to God who was calling me in with the Holy Spirit of His Son, Jesus Christ.

It was a decision I will never regret, and one that many others cherish in their thankful hearts.

How about you? Have the persistent flames of conviction been burning inside you? Perhaps you have been keenly aware that you need God. Maybe you have tried in many ways to suppress the feelings, yet they simply will not go away. Have your unsuccessful attempts to drown the flames of conviction left you feeling bewildered and troubled? If so, I have great news! God is calling you in!

The troubling unrest you feel is described in 2 Corinthians 7:10 as a "godly sorrow," which "produces repentance." It is the source I used for the following lyric that I hope will encourage you to embrace the conviction as your ally.

Oh, Blessed Sorrow

Like a fever on the brow
That tells of pain that looms within
A godly sorrow in the soul
Warns the wayward heart of sin

Oh, blessed sorrow
Sacred flame
Kindled by transgression
Oh, Blessed sorrow
Fire of shame
Leads me to confession
Leads me to salvation

Oh, what a gift, this burning dread
That calls the sin sick to the cross
And there the healer loves and forgives
And keeps the soul from suff'ring loss

Oh, blessed sorrow
Sacred flame
Kindled by transgression
Oh, blessed sorrow
Fire of shame
Leads me to confession
Leads me to salvation[1]

As you consider God's call, you can be especially glad that His intentions for drawing any of us to Himself are quite different than the reason I enticed the deer to come to me. I called the buck in for the sole purpose of taking its life. God calls us to Himself to give us eternal life! The very familiar passage in John 3:16-17 reveals His purpose for extending the invitation for us to come to Him: "For God so loved the world that He gave His only begotten Son, that whoever believes in Him shall not perish, but have eternal life. For God did not send the Son into the world to judge the world, but that the world might be saved through Him." And the apostle Peter comforts all who are being called by the Holy Spirit of God: "[The Lord] is patient toward you, not wishing for any to perish but for all to come to repentance" (2 Peter 3:9).

God wants to *give* you life, not take it from you. John 10:10 says of those who go to God through Christ, "The thief comes only to steal and kill and destroy; I came that they might have life, and have it abundantly." Furthermore, Jesus said, "I am the way, and the truth, and the life; no one comes to the Father but through Me" (John 14:6). If you are aware that God is calling to you from the midst of the guilt that burns in your spirit, don't walk away from Him. If you do, you may never know the calm that comes only through knowing you are at peace with God. The source of that divine comfort is explained in the apostle Paul's writing to the Romans:

> Therefore, having been justified by faith, we have peace with God through our Lord Jesus Christ...and we exult in hope of the glory of God....
>
> And hope does not disappoint, because the love of God has been poured out within our hearts through the Holy Spirit who was given to us. For while we were still helpless, at the right time Christ died for the ungodly....God demonstrates His own love toward us, in that while we were yet sinners, Christ died for us. Much more then, having now been justified by His blood, we shall be saved from the wrath of God through Him (Romans 5:1,5-6,8-9).

Knowing you are at peace with God comes through accepting the invitation to embrace His only begotten Son. That call, my friend, is well worth heeding.

> Today, if you would hear His voice,
> do not harden your hearts.
> Psalm 95:7-8

Notes

Chapter 2: Crooked Bows

1. Steve Chapman, "The Pocket," from the CD "At the Potter's House," Steve & Annie Chapman, SACD-110, Times & Seasons Music/BMI/2000.
2. Kenny Johnson, "Playing Baseball with Jesus," from the CD "Picture This," Kenny & Donna Johnson/CD No. 6. Used by permission, www.kennyand donnajohnson.com.

Chapter 3: Deer Already in the Heart

1. Steve Chapman, "The Mark," Times & Seasons Music/BMI.

Chapter 4: Deer Don't Talk

1. Steve Chapman, "Deer Don't Talk," Times & Seasons Music/BMI/2006.

Chapter 5: "Instandity"

1. William K. Kirkpatrick, *Psychological Seduction, the Failure of Modern Psychology* (Nashville: Nelson, 1983), p. 67.

Chapter 7: Don't Unpack Your Bags

1. Steve Chapman, "Don't Unpack Your Bags," from the CD "That Way Again," Steve & Annie Chapman/SACD-126, Times & Seasons Music/BMI/2005.

Chapter 10: Dream Coming True

1. Steve Chapman, "Dream Coming True," Times & Seasons Music/BMI/2006.
2. James Alley, "He Never Did Anything," James Alley words/Steve Chapman—music/Times & Seasons Music/BMI.

Chapter 11: Turtle on a Fence Post

1. Steve Chapman, "Psalm 91:7."

Chapter 12: First-Time Caller

1. Steve Chapman, "Blessed Sorrow," from the CD "That Way Again," Steve & Annie Chapman/SACD 126, Times & Seasons Music, Inc/BMI/2004.

About the Author

Steve's love of hunting began in his early teens on a weekend when one of his dad's church members invited him to tag along on an October squirrel hunt. Archery is his first choice for use in the field, followed by muzzle loader, and then pistol or rifle. To date, according to Steve's calculations, he's entered the woods before daylight on over a thousand mornings and hopes to continue that trend for many more years!

Proudly claiming West Virginia as his home state, Steve grew up as the son of a preacher. He met his wife, Annie, in junior high school in 1963. In March 1975, they married after dating a few months and settled in Nashville, Tennessee. There they raised their son and daughter, Nathan and Heidi. When Nathan and Heidi married, Steve and Annie enthusiastically accepted their new daughter-in-law and son-in-law, and now they get to dote on the newest member of the family—their granddaughter, Lily.

Steve is president of S&A Family, Inc., an organization formed to oversee the production of the Chapmans' recorded music. They've had "family life" as the theme of their lyrics since they began singing together in 1980. As Dove Award-winning artists, their schedule sends them to over 100 cities a year to present concerts that feature songs from more than 15 recorded projects.

For a list of available products (CDs/cassettes/videos/ books) or more information about the Chapmans and their ministry, please write to

S&A Family, Inc.
PO Box 337
Pleasant View, TN 37146

or check out their website:

www.steveandanniechapman.com